BLOCKCHAIN TECHNOLOGY

How Blockchain will Change the World

A Guide for Beginners

By

Alex Kim

TABLE OF CONTENTS

BLOCKCHAIN EXPLAINED

It is very probable that anyone reading this book has heard of the blockchain and has a basic idea of its huge potential. With the advent of Bitcoin in the year 2008, the world has launched a new concept that could revolutionize the whole of society. This should affect all sectors, including finance, government, and the media. Some describe it as a revolution, while another school of thought says it will be an evolution, and it will take several years before the concrete benefits of blockchain will come to fruition. This is true to some extent, but in my opinion, the revolution has already begun. Many large organizations around the world are already developing proof of concept using blockchain technology, and their potential is now fully recognized. Some organizations are still in the early stages of research but are expected to grow faster as technology becomes more advanced. This technology also has an impact on current technologies and is capable of changing them at a fundamental level.

Distributed Systems

Understanding distributed systems is crucial to understanding the blockchain because it is actually a distributed system. More specifically, it is a decentralized system. Distributed systems are an IT paradigm in which two or more people work together to achieve a common result. They are modeled so that end users see them as a single logical platform. The node can be explained as an individual player in a distributed system. All nodes can send and receive messages. Nodes can be loyal, malicious, or faulty and have their own processor and memory. A node that can show arbitrary behavior is also called a Byzantine node. This arbitrary behavior can be intentionally malicious and affect the operation of the network. In general, any unexpected behavior of a network node can be classified as Byzantine.

The main challenge of a distributed distribution system is the coordination between nodes and fault tolerances. Even if some nodes become faulty or the network connections are broken, the distributed system must tolerate it and continue to work without problems to achieve the desired result. It has been a major field of research for many years, and several algorithms and mechanisms have been proposed to overcome these problems. Distributed systems are difficult to understand because the proven theorem is known as PAC theory and indicates that a distributed system may not have all the desired properties at the same time.

CAP Theorem

This is also known as the Bremore Theorem, originally introduced by Eric Brewer as an assumption in 1998; In 2002, Seth Gilbert and Nancy Lynch proved this as a theorem. The theorem shows that any distributed system cannot simultaneously have a tolerance of coherence, availability, and partition:

• Consistency is a feature that ensures that all nodes in a distributed system have one copy of the latest data.

• Availability means that the system in operation, available for use, accepts incoming requests and responds, if necessary, with fault-free data.

• Partition tolerance ensures that if a node group fails, the distributed system continues to function properly.

It has been shown that a distributed system cannot have all three of these properties simultaneously. However, it seems strange that the blockchain manages to achieve all these properties, or does it really? The CAP theorem, as related to blockchains will be talked about later in this book.

Replication is used to obtain fault tolerance. This is a common and widely utilized method for achieving it. Consistency is reached by utilizing consensus algorithms to ensure that all nodes have the same copy of the data. This is also called state machine replication. Blockchain is basically a method for performing machine state replication. Generally, a node can find two types of failures: when a failed node is simply blocked and can produce malicious or inconsistent behavior. It is a difficult kind to deal with as it can be confusing due to misinformation.

Byzantine Generals problem

Before discussing consensus in distributed systems, historical events are presented as precursors to the development of effective and practical consensus mechanisms. Paul Baran introduced cryptographic signatures in September 1962 in his article on distributed communication networks. It is this document that first introduced the concept of decentralized networks. Then, in 1982, Lamport et al. suggested a mental experiment whereby a group of military generals leading different parts of the Byzantine army intended to attack or withdraw from the city.

The only means of communication between them is the messenger, and they must agree to attack at the same time to win. The problem is that few or more generals can be traitors and can convey the wrong message. Therefore, it is necessary to find a viable mechanism for agreement between the generals, even in the presence of treacherous generals, so that an attack can occur simultaneously. As an analogy to distributed systems, generals can be considered nodes, traitors can be considered byzantine (malicious) nodes, and the messenger can be considered a communication channel amongst the generals.

In 1999, this problem was solved by Castro and Liskov, who introduced the Byzantine error tolerance algorithm and the practical tolerance algorithm (PBFT). Later, in 2009, the first practical implementation was achieved with the introduction of bitcoin, where the Proof of Work (PoW) algorithm emerged as a mechanism for reaching consensus.

Consensus

Consensus is a procedure of agreement between distributing nodes on a last state of data. So as to achieve consensus, various calculations can be utilized. It is anything but difficult to agree between two nodes (for instance, in customer server frameworks). However, when multiple nodes are taking an interest in a disseminated framework, and they have to agree on a solitary value.

This concept of accomplishing consensus between multiple nodes is known as appropriated consensus.

Consensus mechanisms

A consensus mechanism is a lot of steps that are taken by all or most nodes so as to agree on a proposed state or value. For over three decades, this concept has been examined by PC researchers in the business world and academia. Consensus mechanisms have, as of late, come into the spotlight and increased in notoriety with the approach of bitcoin and blockchain. There exist numerous requirements that must be met so as to give the ideal outcomes in a consensus mechanism. Here are their requirements with brief portrayals:

Agreement: all legit nodes settle on a similar value.

End: all legitimate nodes end execution of the consensus procedure and, in the long run, arrive at a decision.

Legitimacy: the value agreed upon by every genuine node must be equivalent to the underlying value proposed by at any rate one honest node.

Deficiency tolerant: the consensus calculation ought to have the option to run in the presence of defective or malignant nodes (Byzantine nodes).

Uprightness: this is where no node settles on the decision more than once. The nodes settle on decisions just once in a solitary consensus cycle.

Types of consensus mechanism

There are different types of consensus mechanism; some normal types are depicted as follows:

• Byzantine fault tolerance-based: with no compute intense operations, for example, halfway hash reversal, this strategy depends on a basic plan of nodes that are distributing marked messages. Inevitably, when a specific number of messages are obtained, an agreement is made.

• Leader-based consensus mechanisms: This sort of mechanism expects nodes to vie for the leader-political election lottery and the node that successes it proposes a final value.

Numerous useful implementations have been proposed, for example, Paxos, the most celebrated convention presented by Leslie Lamport in 1989. In Paxos, nodes are relegated different jobs, for example, proposer, acceptor, and learner. Nodes or procedures are named copies, and consensus is achieved in the presence of flawed nodes by agreement among a majority of nodes. Another option to Paxos is RAFT, which works by appointing any of three roles – follower, candidate, or leader – to the nodes. A leader is chosen after an applicant node achieves enough votes, and all progressions currently need the approval of the leader, who submits the proposed changes once replication on the majority of supporter nodes is completed.

THE HISTORY OF BLOCKCHAIN

Blockchain was introduced with the bitcoin innovation in 2008, then its practical implementation in 2009. Bitcoin needs to be introduced quickly for this part, as there is a whole bitcoin section later, but it is also important to refer to bitcoin in light of the fact that without it, the blockchain context is incomplete. The concept of electronic money or digital currency is not new. Since the 1980s, there have been electronic money conventions modeled by David Chaum.

In the same way that understanding the concepts of distributed systems is fundamentally about understanding blockchain innovation, the ability to use electronic money is so essential to building the first surprisingly effective use of blockchain: bitcoin or fully digital currency concepts hypothetically in distributed systems; for example, consensus algorithms laid the foundations for the practical implementation of bitcoin work test algorithms. In addition, ideas have been prepared for several parcels of electronic money to increase cryptocurrency, explicitly bitcoin.

The Concept of Electronic Cash

Fundamental issues that should be attended to in e-cash systems are responsibility and secrecy. David Chaum tended to both of these issues in his fundamental paper in 1984 by presenting two cryptographic activities, in particular blind signatures and secret sharing. Right now, it is adequate to state that blind signatures permit marking a report without really observing it, and secret sharing is a concept that permits recognition of utilization of a similar e-cash token twice (twofold spending).

After these different conventions were developed, for example, Chaum, Fiat, and Naor (CFN), there were e-cash plots that presented obscurity and twofold spending location. Brand e-cash is another framework that enhanced CFN that made it progressively productive and introduced the concept of security reduction to exposed explanations about the e-cash scheme. Security reduction is a method used in cryptography to demonstrate that a specific algorithm is secure by utilizing another issue as an examination. In another aspect, a cryptographic security algorithm is as difficult to break as some other difficult issue; in this manner, by examination, it may very well be reasoned that the cryptographic security algorithm is secure as well.

An alternative but applicable concept called hashcash was introduced by Adam Back in 1997 as a PoW framework to control email spam. The thought is very straightforward: if legitimate users need to send messages, at which point they are needed to compute a hash as a proof that they have spent a sensible measure of computing resources before sending the email. Creating a hashcash is a high computational process, but it does not prevent the legitimate user from sending emails since the typical number of messages a legitimate user has to send is very small. Again, spammers have to send emails, usually thousands of times, and it is impossible to calculate hashcash for all messages, which is expensive; as a result, this mechanism can be used to block spam. Hashcash requires many computing resources to be calculated, but it is urgent to confirm this. The confirmation is provided by the user who receives the email. Hashcash promotes its use in the bitcoin extraction process. The idea of using computer puzzles or evaluating pricing puzzles for preventing email spams was first introduced in 1992 by Moni Naor and Cynthia Dwork.

The appraisal function is the name of the actual skills that will be calculated before access to the property is granted. Subsequently, Adam Back independently created the hashcash in 1997. Wei Dai introduced b-money in 1998 and came up with the idea of making money by solving computer puzzles, such as hashcash, for example. It depends on the distributed system in which each node maintains its list of transactions. Another of Nick Szabo's comparative idea, called BitGold, was introduced in 2005 and also suggested solving puzzles that govern computer-based currencies. Hal Finney introduced the concept of crypto money in 2005, joining the ideas of b-money and hashcash, but it still depends on puzzling power.

There were many problems with the plans described above in the unworkable sections. These issues run from no unmistakable arrangement of disagreements between nodes to dependence on a central trusted in outsider and trusted timestamping. In 2009, the main practical implementation of a digital currency named bitcoin was introduced; for the absolute first time, it tackled the issue of distributed consensus in a trustless system. It utilizes open key cryptography with hashcash as PoW to give a safe, controlled, and decentralized technique for stamping computerized cash. The key development is the idea of an ordered rundown of squares made out of transactions and cryptographically verified by the PoW mechanism. Taking a look at all the previously mentioned innovations and their history, it is anything but difficult to perceive how ideas and concepts from electronic cash plots and distributed systems were joined together to create bitcoin and what presently is known as blockchain.

INTRODUCTION TO BLOCKCHAIN

There are different definitions of blockchain; it relies upon how you look at it. In the event that you take a look at it from a business point of view, it very well may be defined in that unique situation. In the event that you take a look at it from a specialized viewpoint, one can characterize it in view of that. Blockchain at its center is a shared distributed record that is cryptographically secure, append-only, permanent (very difficult to change), and updateable just by means of agreement or consensus among peers. It can be seen as a layer of a distributed shared system running on top of the Internet. It is undifferentiated from SMTP, HTTP, or FTP running on top of TCP/IP.

Enthusiasm for blockchain technology has taken off over the most recent couple of years and, when dismissed by some as nerd money from a digital money perspective or as something that was not so much viewed as beneficial, it is currently being investigated by the biggest organizations and associations around the globe with a lot of money being spent so as to embrace and try different things with this technology.

The system view of a blockchain

From a business perspective, a blockchain can be defined as a stage whereby peers can trade values utilizing transactions without the requirement for a focal disclosed mediator. This is a powerful concept, and once you comprehend it, you will understand the tsunamic capability of blockchain technology. This permits blockchain to be a decentralized consensus mechanism where no single authority is accountable for the database. A block is just a choice of transactions packaged together so as to sort them intelligently. It is comprised of transactions, and its size is variable, relying upon the type and design of the blockchain being used. A reference to a previous block is additionally remembered for the block except if it's a genesis block. A genesis block is a principal block in the blockchain that was hardcoded at the time the blockchain began. The structure of a block is additionally reliant on the type and design of a blockchain, however, for the most part, there are a couple of attributes that are basic to the usefulness of a block, for example, the block header, pointers to previous blocks, the timestamp, nonce, transaction counter, transactions, and different attributes.

Different Technical Definitions of Blockchains

• Blockchain is a decentralized consensus component. In a blockchain, all companions, at last, reach a consensus concerning the state of a transaction.

• Blockchain is a circulated, shared record. It can be seen as a typical record of transactions. The transactions are requested and collected into blocks. This present reality model depends on private databases that each affiliation maintains; however, the circulated record can fill in as a lone wellspring of truth for all connections that are using the blockchain.

- Blockchain is an information structure; it is basically an associated summary that uses hash pointers instead of conventional pointers. Hash pointers are utilized to point to the previous block.

Blockchain Elements

In this section, the conventional elements of blockchain are explained.

Addresses

Addresses are unique identifiers that are utilized in a transaction on the blockchain to signify senders and recipients. An address is normally a public key or derived from a public key. While addresses can be reused by a similar user, addresses themselves are unique. Practically speaking, a solitary user may not use a similar address again and produce another one for every transaction. This recently created address will be unique. Bitcoin is, in actuality, a pseudonymous framework. End users are normally not easily identifiable, but rather, some investigation in de-anonymizing bitcoin users has demonstrated that users can be identified effectively. As a decent practice, it is proposed that users produce another address for every transaction to abstain from connecting transactions to the user, hence maintaining a strategic distance from being identified.

Transaction

A transaction is the key unit of a blockchain. A transaction speaks to a transfer of significant value, starting with one address then onto the next.

Block

A block is made out of numerous transactions and some different elements, for example, the preceding block (hash pointer), nonce, and timestamp.

Shared network

As the name infers, this is a network topology whereby all users can communicate with one another.

Scripting or programming language.

This element performs different activities on a transaction. Transaction scripts are predefined sets of directions for nodes to transfer symbols, starting with one address, then onto the next, and perform different functions. Turing complete programming language is an alluring element of blockchains; so, the security of such languages is a key inquiry and a zone of significant and continuous research.

Virtual machine

This is an increase of a transaction script. A virtual machine grants Turing complete code to be run on a blockchain (as smart contracts); however, a transaction script can be confined in its action. Virtual machines are not accessible on all blockchains;

regardless, unique blockchains use virtual machines to run programs, for instance, Ethereum Virtual Machine (EVM) and Chain Virtual Machine (CVM).

State machine

A blockchain can be seen as a state change instrument whereby a state is balanced from its hidden structure to the following and over the long haul to the final structure because of a transaction execution and approval process by nodes.

Nodes

A node in a blockchain mastermind performs various functions depending form it takes. A node can propose and endorse transactions and perform mining to empower consensus and secure the blockchain. This is done by following a consensus convention. (this is PoW). Nodes can, in this manner, perform various functions, for instance, direct installment check (lightweight nodes), validators, and various other functions depending on the type of the blockchain used and the activity selected to the node.

Smart contracts

These schemes run over the blockchain and exemplify the business rationale to be executed when certain conditions are met. The smart understanding feature isn't accessible in all blockchains, yet is now transforming into an altogether alluring element because of the flexibility and power it provides for the blockchain applications.

FEATURES OF BLOCKCHAIN

A blockchain performs different functions. These are discussed below in detail.

Distributed consensus

Distributed consensus is the major support of a blockchain. This empowers a blockchain to introduce a solitary form of integrity that is settled upon by all parties without the necessity of a focal position.

Transaction verification

Any transactions initiated from nodes on the blockchain are confirmed dependent on a foreordained arrangement of rules, and just legitimate transactions are chosen for incorporation in a block.

Platforms for smart contracts

A blockchain is where projects can maintain and execute business logic in the interest of the users. As clarified before, not all blockchains have a mechanism to execute smart contracts; so, this is presently a truly alluring feature. Transferring value between blockchains empowers the transfer of value between its users by means of tokens. Tokens can be thought of as a transporter of value.

Creating digital currency

This is a discretionary feature depending on the sort of

blockchain used. A blockchain can produce cryptographic money as an incentive to its miners who approve the transactions and spend resources so as to verify the blockchain.

Smart property

Just because it is conceivable to link a computerized or physical asset to the blockchain in a permanent way, with the end goal that it can't be guaranteed by any other person, you are in total control of your asset, and it can't be twofold spent or twofold claimed. Contrast it and a computerized music file, for instance, which can be duplicated ordinarily with no control; on a blockchain, if you possess it, nobody else can guarantee it except if you choose to transfer it to somebody. This feature has expansive ramifications, particularly in Digital Rights Management (DRM) and electronic cash systems, where twofold spend discovery is a key necessity. The twofold spend issue was first tackled in bitcoin.

Provider of security

Blockchain depends on demonstrated cryptographic technology that guarantees the integrity and accessibility of data. By and large, confidentiality isn't provided because of the requirements of transparency. This has become a fundamental hindrance for its flexibility by budgetary establishments and different businesses that need privacy and confidentiality of transactions. Accordingly, it is being researched effectively, and there is, as of now, some great advancement made. It could be contended that much of the time, confidentiality isn't really needed, and transparency is favored. For example, in bitcoin, confidentiality isn't really required; nonetheless, it is alluring in certain situations. Research shows that it is extremely ready, and now significant advancement has been made towards giving confidentiality and privacy on the blockchain. A later example is Zcash, which will be examined in more detail in later parts. Other security services, for instance, nonrepudiation and verification, are likewise provided by blockchain as all actions are verified by utilizing private keys and advanced marks.

Unchanging nature

This is another major feature of blockchain: records once added onto the blockchain are unchanging. There is the probability of moving back the progressions, but this is viewed as practically difficult to do as it will require an unreasonably expensive measure of registering resources. For example, in many alluring cases of bitcoin in the event that a noxious user needs to change the past blocks, at that point, it would require processing the PoW again for each one of those blocks that have just been added to the blockchain. This trouble makes the records on a blockchain basically changeless.

Uniqueness

This feature of blockchain guarantees that each transaction is unique and has not been spent. This is particularly applicable in cryptographic forms of money where much attractive discovery and evasion of double-spending are a major requirement.

Smart contracts

Blockchain enables a platform to run smart contracts. These are robotized self-governing projects that live on the blockchain and encapsulate business logic and code so as to execute a necessary function when certain conditions are met. This is, in fact, a progressive feature of blockchain as it permits adaptability, programmability, and much attractive control of actions that users of blockchain need to perform as indicated by their particular business requirements.

Recognizing the Potential

This step deepens our understanding of the function of the blockchain by considering a specific type of distributed system: a peer-to-peer network. As a result, it will aid you in understanding why blockchain technology is so popular with technologists and business professionals. This step also points to the main domain of the application, where the blockchain must provide the highest value. In addition, it addresses some of the significance of the peer-to-peer systems in the real sense.

The Metaphor

Can you recollect the last time you purchased a CD at a music store or department store? Most people haven't bought a CD for a long time because the music industry been revolutionized. Today, people download individual songs from music portals, share MP3s with colleagues, or make use of music streams on their smartphones instead of buying CDs. This change began with the emergence of software that allows users to share their music files with one another. But what makes this software so special?

This system, which is most interesting, is interaction with colleagues, the exchange of information with a person at the end of the street. – Shawn Fanning, co-founder of Napster

What Fanning and his colleagues invented was a system of sharing music among peers. In the late 1990s, this software marked the beginning of a new era for the established commercial model of the music industry. This step explains the rise of Napster, the decline in CD sales, and the turnaround of the music niche, which leveraged the power of blockchain.

How a Peer-to-Peer System Disrupted a Whole Industry

The music business has worked for quite a while in this manner: musicians made contracts with studios, which recorded the tunes, created and showcased the music records on a variety of media (e.g., vinyl, tape, or CD), which thus were offered to the clients through a variety of appropriation channels, including retail establishments and particular shops. The studios really worked as intermediaries among musicians and people who appreciate tuning in to music. Music studios could maintain their job as intermediaries because of their selective information and abilities in delivering, marketing, and conveying records. In any case, in the first decade of the 2000s, the world wherein the music studios worked changed significantly.

The digitalization of music, the accessibility of recording gear at moderate costs, the developing spread of the use of PCs, and the rise of the Internet made music studios nonessential. The three functions of music studios—delivering, marketing, and dispersing records—should be possible by the craftsmen and the shoppers themselves. Napster assumed a significant job in the substitution of the music studios as intermediaries. With Napster, people never again depended on the music studios to get the most recent hits. It was conceivable to share singular music documents with people everywhere throughout the world without the need to purchase any CDs. The distributed methodology of Napster, really as a sort of a computerized sharing bazaar for mp3 records, gave purchasers access to a more extensive scope of music than at any other time, making the music studios mostly superfluous and causing them huge misfortunes.

The Potential of Peer-to-Peer Systems.

The Napster case let us know that peer-to-peer systems can possibly reshape entire businesses dependent on a basic thought: supplanting the go-between with peer-to-peer corporations. On account of the music industry, the customary studios and their advertising and appropriation channels that went about as the brokers among specialists and consumers have been supplanted by peer-to-peer document sharing systems. The significant qualities that made the music industry so vulnerable to being supplanted by peer-to-peer systems are the digitization idea of music and the low expenses of replicating and transferring information. The intensity of peer-to-peer systems isn't restricted to the music industry. Every industry that, for the most part, goes about as a broker among makers and clients of digitization or digital goods and administrations is vulnerable to being supplanted by a peer-to-peer system. This announcement may sound somewhat far-fetched; however, you may find numerous go-betweens for digitization and digital goods and administrations around you once you perceive the biggest of all: the financial industry.

What do you have in your bank account or on your credit or charge card? Is it truly money? The money you possess has been transformed into digital bits and bytes quite a while in the past. Just a modest quantity of real money exists as physical banknotes and coins. By far, most of the world's money and resources exist as digital bits and bytes in the concentrated data innovation systems of the financial industry. Banks and numerous different players of the financial industry are only brokers among makers and consumers of bits and bytes that turn a profit with our riches. The demonstration of obtaining, loaning, or transferring money starting with one account then onto the next is only the transfer of digital money used by go-betweens, likewise called middle people. It is astonishing what number of go-betweens are associated with apparently basic exchanges (e.g., transferring money starting with one bank account then onto the next one of every an alternate country involves up to five brokers, which all need their processing time and costs). Therefore, something as basic as transferring a measure of money starting with one bank account then onto the next in an alternate country involves a long processing time and acquires high exchange costs. In a peer-to-peer system, a similar transfer would be a lot more straightforward, and it would require some investment and expenses since it could be prepared as what it seems to be: a transfer of bytes and bits between two peers or hubs, separately.

The benefit of peer-to-peer systems over unified systems is that immediate associations happen between authoritative accomplices rather than aberrant communications through a broker; subsequently, there is less processing time and lower costs. The benefits of peer-to-peer systems are not restricted to money transfer. Each industry that, for the most part, goes about as a mediator among makers and clients of digitization or digital goods and administrations is vulnerable to being supplanted by a peer-to-peer system. As digitalization proceeds, an ever-increasing number of things of regular day to day existence and an expanding measure of goods and administrations will become digitized and will profit by the efficiencies of peer-to-peer systems. Backers of peer-to-peer systems contend that practically all parts of our life will be influenced by the development of digitalization and peer-to-peer systems, for example, installments, savings, loans, protection, issuance, and approval of birth certifications, driving licenses, travel papers, identification cards, proof of qualifications, and licenses and work contracts. The greater part of them as of now exist in digital structure in combined systems run by establishments that are nothing other than a mediator between normal providers and clients.

Terminology and the Link to the Blockchain

After you have discovered the potential of peer-to-peer systems, it is necessary to clarify the terminology of the problem domain and to discuss its relation to the blockchain. In particular, the below points ought to be discussed:

- The definition of a peer-to-peer system

- The architecture of a peer-to-peer systems

- The link between a peer-to-peer systems and a blockchain

THE DEFINITION OF A PEER-TO-PEER SYSTEM

Peer-to-peer systems are distributed programming systems that comprise of nodes (singular computers), which make their computational resources (e.g., processing power, stockpiling limit, or data conveyance) straightforwardly accessible to another. When joining a peer-to-peer system, users transform their computers into nodes of the system that are equivalent to their privileges and jobs. In spite of the fact that users may vary regarding the resources they contribute, every one of the nodes in the system has the equivalent functional ability and duty. Consequently, the computers of all users are the two providers and consumers of resources. For instance, in a peer-to-peer document sharing system, the individual records are put away on the users' machines. At the point when somebody needs to download a document in such a system, the person in question is downloading it from someone else's machine, which could be the nearby neighbor or somebody found across the world.

Architecture of Peer-to-Peer Systems

Peer-to-peer systems are distributed computer systems by development since they are made of individual nodes that offer their computational resources, among others. In any case, there are likewise peer-to-peer systems that still use elements of centralization. Centralized peer-to-peer systems maintain focal nodes to encourage the collaboration between peers, to maintain indexes that portray the administrations offered by the peer nodes, or to perform look-ups and to distinguish proof of the nodes. Centralized peer-to-peer systems commonly use a mixture of architecture. Such architecture permits consolidating the benefits of centralized and distributed registering. Then again, purely distributed peer-to-peer systems don't have any element of focal control or coordination. Consequently, all nodes in those systems play out similar errands, acting both as suppliers and consumers of resources and administrations. A case of a centralized peer-to-peer system is Napster, which kept up the main database of all nodes associated with the system and the tunes accessible on these nodes.

The Link Between Peer-to-Peer Systems and Blockchain

The blockchain can be viewed as an apparatus for achieving and maintaining integrity in distributed systems. Purely distributed peer-to-peer systems can utilize the blockchain so as to achieve and to maintain system integrity. Thus, the link between purely distributed peer-to-peer systems and the blockchain is its use for achieving and maintaining integrity in purely distributed systems.

The Potential of the Blockchain

The connection between purely distributed peer-to-peer systems to the blockchain is that the previous uses the former as a device to achieve and maintain integrity. Subsequently, the contention that clarifies the energy about and the potential of the blockchain is:

Purely distributed peer-to-peer systems have an immense business potential as they can supplant centralized systems and change entire ventures because of disintermediation. Since a distributed peer-to-peer systems may use the blockchain for achieving and maintaining integrity, the blockchain becomes significant also. Notwithstanding, the significant truth that energizes people is the disintermediation. The blockchain is just a necessary task that achieves that.

WHY BLOCKCHAIN IS NEEDED

This section explains the problem that the blockchain is supposed to solve and why solving this problem is important. This stage also demystifies your understanding of the problem domain in which the blockchain is located, the environment in which it contributes the most value, and its relation to trust, integrity, and the management of ownership. At the end of this section, you would have gained a deeper understanding of the purpose of the blockchain, and you will end up with a differentiated understanding of the term blockchain itself.

The Metaphor

Many languages have a pictorial saying to describe the situation when someone tries to organize a chaotic group of individuals. For instance, in English one, would describe such a situation as trying to herd cats, as it demonstrates the challenges of herding a group of obstinate and intractable animals that do not accept or even recognize a central authority. Does the problem of trying to manage a group of individuals who do not accept or recognize a central authority sound familiar? It happens that this is the same situation as a purely distributed peer-to-peer system, which consists of individual and independent nodes with no kind of central control or coordination. This step explains the key challenge of solely distributed peer-to-peer systems and how it relates to the blockchain.

Trust and Integrity in Peer-to-Peer Systems

Trust and integrity are two sides of the same coin. In the niche of software systems, integrity is a non-functional aspect of a system that must be secure, complete, consistent, correct, and free from corruption and error. Trust is also the deep belief of people in the reliability, truth, or ability of someone or something without evidence, evidence, or research. Confidence is given in advance and will increase or decrease depending on the results of the interactions continuously. As for peer systems, this means that people will join and continue to contribute to the system if they believe it and if the results of their ongoing interaction with the system validate and strengthen their confidence. System integrity is required to meet customer expectations and build confidence in the system. If the system does not enhance user confidence due to lack of integrity, users will abandon it, which will eventually cause its extinction.

Because of the importance of trust for the existence of a peer-to-peer system, the big question is how to achieve and maintain integrity in a purely distributed peer-to-peer system. Achieving and maintaining integrity in cleanly distributed systems depends on many factors, the most important being:

- Knowledge about the number of peers or nodes

- Knowledge about the trustworthiness of the peers

The chances of acquiring integrity in a distributed peer-to-peer system are greater if the number of nodes and their reliability is known. This situation is comparable to managing a private club with high moral standards and using a rigorous registration process for new members. However, the worst circumstances to achieve integrity in a distributed (peer-to-peer) system occur when the number of nodes and their reliability is unknown. This is the case when you use a point-to-point system cleanly distributed on the Internet, open to all.

Integrity Threats in Peer-to-Peer Systems

In simple terms, one can consider two major integrity threats in peer-to-peer systems:

- Technical failures

- Malicious peers

Technical Failures

Peer-to-peer systems consist of the individual computers of their users communicating over the network. All software and hardware components of a computer system, like any component of a computer network, have an imminent risk of failure or error. Therefore, every distributed system must accidentally face the problem that its components may corrupt or produce erroneous results.

Malicious Peers

Malicious members are another threat to integrity in peer

systems. This source of lack of reliability is not a technical problem, but a problem caused by the goals of people who choose to use the system for their own purposes. You could say that this threat is more to do with sociology and group dynamics than technology. Dishonest and wicked peers are the most serious threat to the peer system because they attack the base on which any peer system is built: trust. When users can no longer trust their peers, they move away and stop providing computer resources to the system. As a result, the number of members will decrease, and the whole system will become less attractive to the remaining members, which will accelerate the decline of the system, which will eventually be completely abandoned.

The Core Problem to Be Meet by the Blockchain

Achieving integrity and trust in the best conditions is easy. The real and main challenge is to achieve integrity and trust in the system distributed under the worst conditions, and this is a problem that blockchain should solve. A central problem that blockchain must solve is to achieve and maintain integrity in a purely distributed point-to-point system, made up of an unknown number of peers with unknown reliability and dependability. This problem is not new. It is a well-known and widespread problem in computer science. Using the military metaphor, the problem is widely discussed as a general Byzantine problem.

DEFINING BLOCKCHAIN

This section will turn your attention to the definition of the term and explain its different usages. This step will present a provisional breakdown of blockchain, which will guide you through the remainder of this book. Finally, this stage explains why the management of ownership is a prominent application case of the blockchain.

In this chapter about the blockchain, the term is used as follows:

• As a name for a data structure

• As a name for an algorithm

• As a name for a group of technologies

• As an umbrella term for the purely distributed peer-to-peer systems with a common application area

A Data Structure

In computer science and software engineering, data structure is a means of organizing data regardless of their specific information content. You can imagine the data structure in terms of the floor plan of an architectural building. Floor plan for the construction of directions that separate and connect space with walls, floors, and stairs, regardless of their particular use. When used as a data structure name, the blockchain refers to the data path in units called blocks. These blocks can be thought of as books. These blocks are linked together like a chain, hence the name blockchain. Words and phrases related to a book are information that needs to be stored. They are written on different pages, rather than being written on a large circuit. The pages are interconnected by their position in the book and page numbers. You can determine if someone has deleted a page from a book by checking that the page numbers continue without leaving a number. In addition, the information is classified on the pages as well. Ordering is an important detail that will be widely used. In addition, the ordering of data blocks in the data structure is performed using a very special numbering system, which is different from page numbering in ordinary books.

An Algorithm

The term algorithm in software engineering refers to a series of instructions that a computer must complete. These instructions often include data structures. When used as an algorithm name, blockchain refers to a sequence of instructions that negotiates the information content of many blockchain data structures in a purely distributed point-to-point system, much like a democratic voting scheme.

A Group of Technologies

When used to designate a set of technologies, blockchain refers to a combination of a data chain structure, a blockchain algorithm, and a combination of cryptographic and security technologies that can be used to ensure integrity in a purely distributed architecture, even systems, regardless of the purpose of the application.

An Umbrella Term for the Purely Distributed Peer-to-Peer Systems with a Common Application Area

Blockchain can also be used as a generic term for purely distributed point-to-point books, using the Blockchain technology suite. Note that in this context, the blockchain refers to a fully distributed system as a whole, not a software unit that is part of a purely distributed system.

Provisional Definition

The following definition is incomplete. Important details that have not yet been submitted are still being lost. But this definition is a transitional step toward a more complete understanding of the term: blockchain is a purely distributed and peer-controlled system that uses a software unit consisting of an algorithm that negotiates the information content of commands commanded, and related data blocks as well as cryptographic and security technologies to achieve and maintain their integrity.

The Role of Managing Ownership

The provisional definition doesn't utter a word about Bitcoin or overseeing responsibility for cash. This may come as a shock since numerous articles and books expounded on the blockchain guarantee that its motivation is to oversee responsibility for monetary standards. In all actuality, overseeing responsibility for cash is an unmistakable and common application instance of the blockchain, yet it isn't the one and only one. The blockchain has a wide and various scope of uses. In any case, there are two reasons why the administration of responsibility for products is the most examined utilization of the blockchain.

To start with, it is the most straightforward to comprehend and to clarify. Second, it is the user type with the most effect on the economy. The idea of proprietorship and the authorization of possession rights are center elements of pretty much every human culture (even a few creatures have the idea of possession and battle about its implementation). A tremendous extent of the exercises of banks, insurance agencies, overseers, legal counselors, courts, specialists, and offices are worried about simply the administration of proprietorship rights or their requirements. Thus, overseeing proprietorship is a multibillion-dollar enterprise, and any specialized development that could change the manner in which we oversee possession will have an enormous effect. Incidentally, the blockchain can surely significantly change the manner in which we oversee possession.

The blockchain as an innovation suite is used for overseeing distributed peer-to-peer systems of records; it can have numerous particular applications, for example, overseeing proprietorship in advanced merchandise or cryptographic monetary standards. So, this book intentionally doesn't consider only one explicit utilization of the blockchain because it is not preferred not to divert the consideration from the center ideas by talking about only one explicit application case in incredible detail. In any case, so as to make it simpler for you to comprehend the blockchain, this book considers the general application instance of overseeing and explaining proprietorship, paying little respect to the particular great whose possession is overseen. Subsequently, the general objective of overseeing and explaining proprietorship will give some psychological direction through your learning way and help to make a psychological image of the blockchain.

Ownership and Witnesses

Have you ever pondered about what makes you the owner of the thing that belongs to you? Probably because in supermarket history, you always think of an apple! So what does an apple owner do in your bag? How can you make sure you didn't steal it at the supermarket? They imagine that they are before a court challenging their so-called apple theft case. How would you confirm that you own an apple? We know that in the example of a supermarket, it would be enough to prove his innocence when no one could check if he stole an apple. However, being released from jail theft does not constitute proof of ownership. Let's continue with the question of proving your property. It would be very helpful if someone could testify that you bought an apple before going to the supermarket. Fortunately, remember the store where you bought the apple, and the employee who sold you the apple is ready to testify.

In any case, you thought little of the examiner. He is conversing with your observer in the interrogation and asking your observer hard inquiries: Can he recall the apple he offered to you? Would he be able to distinguish the particular apple he offered to you as the apple found in your sack? Would he be able to distinguish you as the individual who purchased that specific apple? Lastly, for what reason does he recollect every one of these subtleties in any case? Would it be able to be conceivable that you paid the observer cash for vouching for your blamelessness? So this boils down to a fundamental rule: having one observer is great, yet having numerous independent observers is the key to persuading the investigator of your blamelessness.

The last point is critical. The more independent observers who vouch for a similar reality, the higher the possibility that this is reality. Things being what they are, this thought will be one of the central ideas of the blockchain.

Foundation of Ownership

Taking the discoveries of the past area to an increasingly conceptual level, one can express that demonstrating proprietorship includes three elements:

- A recognizable proof of the proprietor

- A recognizable proof of the item being possessed

- A mapping of the proprietor to the item

The declaration of witnesses achieves these. Truly, observers have regularly been the main wellspring of explaining these elements. Notwithstanding, depending on oral declarations of witnesses is tedious. Subsequently, these elements have been supplanted by records given by reliable elements. These days, we can distinguish people with ID cards, birth declarations, and driver's licenses. Sequential numbers, creation dates, generation endorsements, or a nitty-gritty description can be used to recognize objects. These reports don't change once they are made because the characters of people and items don't change.

The mapping among proprietors and items is normally completed with a record or register. This isn't a report that remains constant once made. Each transfer of possession should be recorded in such a register because an obsolete register or record can't be a reliable observer for affirming proprietorship. The significance of having an exceptional and precise overseen register has prompted the advancement of unique organizations in numerous social orders. The more significant specific sorts of items are, the higher the possibility for the presence of an administration directed record that archives the responsibility for objects. A large portion of these records is available to everybody so as to make it simple to confirm possession and give simple access to explain proprietorship. You may do some exploration all alone to distinguish a portion of these records in your country and to what they uphold. I discovered records for reporting responsibility for domain, licenses, boats, planes, and organizations. I even discovered registers for relationships, births, and deaths.

A Short Detour to Security

There are three majorly used security-related concepts that need to be explained in more detail, as their meaning as related to the field of software systems might be a bit different from their common usage:

- Identification

- Authentication

- Authorization

The importance and interrelation of these three ideas can be shown in a real-world example. Maybe you endeavor to purchase a jug of wine in a liquor shop. Liquor shops are not permitted to offer alcohol to individuals who are underage. How does the liquor shop guarantee that it sells wine just to the right people? The liquor shop achieves this by utilizing identification, authentication, and approval. Also, here is a clarification on how this function.

Identification

Identification simply means to claim to be someone by stating a name or whatever else that could be used as an identifier. In the liquor shop example, one could say to be someone in particular by stating a name. Identification doesn't prove that you really are who you claim to be. Identification doesn't include the proof that you are not underage. Identification just means claiming to be someone in particular.

Authentication

The motivation behind authentication is to prevent someone

from claiming to be someone else. Authentication means confirming or demonstrating that you really are who you claim to be. This proof can be demonstrated by something you have or something you realize that can fill in as proof that you really are who you claim to be (e.g., an ID card, a driver's license, or a few subtleties of the life of the person you claim to be). It is significant that the proof of your claimed identity is uniquely associated with you (e.g., a photograph of your face, a unique mark, or something else that identifies you uniquely). In the liquor shop example, this means you can prove that you really are who you claimed to be by demonstrating a driver's license that contains a photograph of you. Contrasting your face and the face appeared on the photograph on the driver's license achieves the verification. In the event that you resemble the person in the photograph of the driver's license, the authentication is fruitful. Something else, the authentication comes up short. Double-checking one's face with respect to the photograph on the driver's license means to prevent someone from utilizing someone else's driver's license.

Authorization

Authorization means giving access to explicit resources or services because of the characteristics or properties of one's identity. Authorization is the result of both a fruitful authentication and an assessment of one's characteristics or rights. In the liquor store example, authorization means to decide whether you are permitted to purchase a bottle of wine dependent on the date of birth shown on your driver's license. The shop assistant will not allow you to buy you a bottle of wine in the event that you are excessively youthful, dependent on the date of birth shown on your driver's license. Note that in this case, the refusal isn't because of a failed authentication. Identification and authentication performed well, and because of the right identification, the shop assistant can identify you as an underage person. Consequently, authorization is consistently the consequence of assessing the characteristics or properties of the recently authenticated identity against certain standards.

Purposes and Properties of a Ledger

The ledger needs to satisfy two contradicting jobs. From one viewpoint, a ledger fills in as a means for proving ownership, which depends on perusing notable data protected in the ledger. Then again, the ledger needs to record any transfer of ownership, which thus infers that new data are created and kept in touch with the ledger. One of the most significant contrasts of these two purposes can be outlined in the contradicting idea of transparency and privacy. Proving ownership is simpler when the ledger is open to anybody. Consequently, transparency is the basis of proving ownership rights likewise as witnesses making a public declaration in court. So, transferring ownership must be only limited to the legal proprietor. So privacy is basically the basis of transferring ownership. Since writing in the ledger means evolving ownership, truth be told, trustful substances ought to be given writing access to ledgers. The clashing powers of transparency versus privacy, proving ownership versus transferring ownership, and perusing the ledger versus writing the ledger can likewise be found in the blockchain. For reasons unknown, the blockchain is a tremendous distributed peer-to-peer system of ledger-like data structures that can be perused by everybody.

Ownership and the Blockchain

A witness as an administration controlled ledger is the key to clarifying ownership of significant merchandise. However, what occurs if such a ledger is harmed or devastated? Or, on the other hand, what occurs if someone liable for refreshing the ledger makes a blunder or falsify it on purpose? In this case, the ledger doesn't reflect reality. This is shocking because everyone accepts that the ledger speaks to the truth, like a witness in court. The issue of having just a single ledger as the hotspot for clarifying ownership can be explained similarly as it has been understood for preliminaries in court. Putting together a decision just with respect to the declaration of one single witness is unsafe since this witness could be exploitative. Having more witnesses is better.

The more independent witnesses who are cross-examined, the higher the possibility that those realities that are reliably referenced among the majority of declarations mirror the truth. This reality can be proved by means of measurements and the law of huge numbers. Having numerous witnesses who independently mention their own objective facts free of shared impacts is the key to this approach to demystifying the truth. Applying this finding to the utilization of a ledger for clarifying ownership is direct: instead of maintaining just one single ledger that could be manufactured, one ought to use a purely distributed peer-to-peer system of ledgers and explain demands concerning ownership on that form of the reality on which the majority of peers concurs.

Characteristics of the Blockchain

The blockchain is a mainly distributed peer-to-peer data store with the following properties:

• Immutable

• Append-only

• Ordered

• Time-stamped

• Open and transparent

• Secure (identification, authentication, and authorization)

• Eventually consistent

These blockchain properties are independent of the specific data stored there. Therefore, from a simplistic point of view, blockchain can be considered as a special type of storage box for digital elements. This will open up a wide variety of blockchain applications.

Generic Application Templates

Depending on the properties of the blockchain and the characteristics of being a generic data warehouse for all types of data, we can suggest the following generic use cases:

- Proof of existence

- Proof of nonexistence

- Proof of time

- Proof of order

- Proof of identity

- Proof of authorship

- Proof of ownership

Proof of Existence

This use of blockchain focuses on storing data for the sole purpose of demonstrating its existence. As a result, this usage does not use interlace functions or timestamp block connections. Practical applications, for example, are case records that should be unique, such as trademarks, patents, license codes, and an Internet or email address.

Proof of Nonexistence

This use of the blockchain sees to the opposite of the proof of existence. It gives ways to verify whether specific entries or items do not exist in the blockchain. Concrete applications of this are the records of complaints, fines, or convictions.

Proof of Time

In this case, not just only the sheer presence of a section in the blockchain is significant but also the time when the passage was added. The blockchain can fulfill that need since the blocks of the blockchain-data-structure store the time when the process of including them began. Applications that profit by the time-stepping capabilities of the blockchain are those that track the event of occasions in time, for example, conveyance or warning following, following of installments, following of orderly opening and shutting of public bidding procedures, and management of forecasts.

Proof of Order

This pattern of use uses the ordering capability of the blockchain. Applications that benefit from that property of the blockchain are those that track the general ordering of occasions, paying little mind to their total time, for example, following application processes, reviewing public bidding procedures, and escrow services. Proving that some occasion was the first or the remnant of a dying breed is a particular example of proof of order. This sort of proof can be significant when resources are designated in a similar order where certain claims or documents are submitted, for example, school or college applications, patent applications, or copyright claims.

Proof of Identity

Proof of identity can be considered a particular case of proof of presence because it proves that a specific identity as of now exists. The blockchain fulfills that use case since it not just stores data that can be used to identify someone or something, yet in addition, it provides essential security concepts for identification and authentication. Solid applications of this use pattern are advanced identity documents for people, creatures, or merchandise. Governments could use such blockchains as part of their e-government methodology for overseeing personal documents, drivers' licenses, or travel papers.

Proof of Authorship

This utilize pattern focuses on proving that a particular person or foundation added certain data to the blockchain. The blockchain can fill that need because it not just stores data that can be identified by its unique cryptographic mark, yet additionally offers essential security concepts, for example, identification, authentication, and authorization. Identification and authentication are important to identify creators and confirm their identity. Authorization is vital in this use case so as to prevent someone from adding data to the blockchain without reserving the privilege to do so. Applications that use this pattern are, for example, electronic distributing, following of content changes in documents, content conveyance, shared altering, and ensuring copyrights.

Proof of Ownership

This use pattern focuses on overseeing and explain ownership. It depends on all recently referenced patterns, for example, proof of presence, proof of order, proof of identity, and proof of initiation together with the three essential security concepts:

identification, authentication, and authorization. Applications that use this use pattern are, for example, systems for overseeing ownership of real domains, vehicles, organization shares, securities, computerized cash, or cryptographic monetary forms.

NICHE USE CASES OF BLOCKCHAIN

The blockchain is agnostic as for the data it stores. Henceforth, the range of data being stored in the blockchain and the range of its application territories are as wide and as assorted as human exercises themselves. Therefore, it is difficult to provide a total diagram of all blockchain applications. Consequently, this section introduces a little choice of cement blockchain application zones in which the blockchain is being used or might be used soon:

• Payments: managing ownership and transfer of advanced fiat monetary standards.

• Cryptocurrencies: managing ownership and creation of advanced instruments of installment that exist independently from any administration, national bank, or other focal foundation.

• Micropayments: transfer of modest quantities of cash that would be excessively expensive by utilizing customary means of transfer.

• Digital assets: managing development, ownership, and transfer of computerized things that have value in their own right or speak to important products in reality.

• Digital identity: proving identity and authentication dependent on unique advanced things.

• Notary services: digitizing, storing, and confirming documents or contracts and proof of ownership or transfer.

• Compliance and review: auditing business exercises of people or organizations in managed ventures in a review track.

• Tax: calculating and gathering charges dependent on transactions or on sole ownership, lessening charge avoidance, or twofold tax collection.

• Voting: creating, appropriating, and checking advanced voting form papers.

• Record management: creation and storing of therapeutic records.

Analyzing Blockchain Applications

Analyzing a blockchain application may become vital in a variety of events, for example, turning into a client of a company that uses the blockchain, putting resources into a blockchain startup, or utilizing a blockchain application in your own company. In these cases, it needs to be decided whether a certain blockchain application is useful or whether it has an unmistakable value. Since the blockchain is a complex, specialized development, it might be trying to get an unmistakable perspective on the capabilities of the product system viable and to make a cognizant buy, venture, or utilization choice. Consequently, it might solicit a few or all from the following questions:

• What kind of blockchain is used?

• Are the requirements for utilizing the blockchain fulfilled?

• What is the added value of utilizing a distributed peer-to-peer system?

• What is the application idea?

• What is the business case?

• How are peers made up for contributing resources to the system?

Are the Requirements for Utilizing the Blockchain Fulfilled?

The blockchain is a majorly distributed peer-to-peer system that comprises of an obscure number of peers of obscure unwavering quality and dependability. Consequently, the main point to be considered when analyzing a solid blockchain application is its architecture and whether the architecture satisfies the conditions for applying the blockchain-technology-suite. It is imperative to discover acceptable responses to the following questions:

• What is the architecture of the system?

• What are the system parts, and how are they associated with each other?

• Is the system basically distributed, or is there a focal portion whose failure can cut down the entire system?

• How do new nodes join the system?

• Can everybody join the system and begin to contribute to computational resources?

• Is there any type of on-boarding process, due steadiness process, or forthright security checking of new nodes that may set up a focal element of control?

• Do all nodes have identical jobs and rights in the system, or do the nodes vary concerning their rights to peruse or compose data?

Responding to these questions will assist you with gaining an essential comprehension of the system and decide if the blockchain-technology-suite is really needed. You could discover that maybe the blockchain system viable is a centralized system.

What Kind of Blockchain Is Used?

Not every single distributed system is open to everybody and granting perusing and writing access to every one of their nodes. There are adaptations of the blockchain that contrast with the designation of perusing and writing access among the nodes. These distinctions affect the architecture and the distributed idea of the system just as on the purpose of the blockchain inside those systems. Consequently, it is essential to discover fulfilling answers to the following questions:

• What kind of blockchain is used (public versus private and permissioned versus permissionless)?

• What rights are confined?

• What gatherings of nodes have which rights?

• Why has the particular kind of blockchain been picked?

• Who determines which rights are given to what assembly of nodes?

• Who makes and upholds the principles in regards to allowing or declining perusing or writing access to the system?

• Who runs the on-boarding process?

• Are there any privacy or adaptability worries in the particular arrangement that could legitimize the confinement of specific rights?

What Is the Added Value of Applying the Purely Peer-to-Peer System?

Both purely distributed peer-to-peer systems and the centralized systems have their very own advantages and disadvantages. Centralized systems are not innately terrible; they simply seek after an alternate compositional concept that serves numerous application cases well overall and still keeps on doing such. With certain characteristics, centralized systems might be more attractive than distributed peer-to-peer systems. This is particularly valid as integrity in purely distributed peer-to-peer systems is famously difficult to maintain and costs extra exertion. Henceforth, one needs valid justifications for picking a distributed peer-to-peer system over a centralized one. While analyzing a solid blockchain application, it is important to find fulfilling answers to the following questions:

• Why was the system executed as a purely distributed peer-to-peer system in any case?

• What are the alternatives?

• What are the advantages of using a purely distributed peer-to-peer architecture over the alternatives, and what are the disadvantages?

• What is the added value of utilizing a distributed peer-to-peer architecture?

• Do the advantages of peer-to-peer architecture exceed the disadvantages?

Asking and demanding the responses to these questions is important to separate the individuals who deliberately pick the distributed peer-to-peer architecture from the individuals who use the blockchain only for utilizing it.

What Is the Application Idea?

Analyzing the architecture of any particular system is important, yet, this doesn't yield answers concerning its application idea and how the system should make added value for its users. It is basic to remember that even the most advanced system architecture can never make up for a weak or poor application idea. The fervor surrounding the blockchain-technology-suite may make it barely noticeably a weak or poor application concept. Henceforth, while analyzing a blockchain application, it is important to discover persuading answers to the following questions:

• What is the aim of the application in any case?

• What is the serious issue area of the system?

• Can the system be related to explicit businesses or sectors, and if so, what are they?

• What kind of administration does the system offer to its users?

• What is the added value of applying this system?

• What kind of nonexclusive blockchain use pattern does the system use?

• Are there any issues with the legitimate acknowledgment of the blockchain in the particular application zone?

• What sorts of data are stored in the blockchain?

• What kinds of tasks or transactions should be possible?

• What kinds of security features are used?

• How do these viewpoints identify with the application idea of the system?

Another important perspective when analyzing blockchain applications is simply the business concept of the software system itself. The creation and activity of any software devour resources and thus cause costs. The blockchain is not new to that. Analyzing the business states of blockchain software is an important advance since numerous products or specialized developments flop because of imperfections in their business concepts. Consequently, it is important to discover clever responses to the following questions:

• What are the costs of buying or utilizing the software?

• What are the variable and fixed costs of running or utilizing the software?

• Who takes care of what costs?

• What license model is used?

• Who receives benefits or who needs to cover misfortunes?

BITCOIN

itcoin started the revolution by introducing the first fully decentralized digital currency, which has proven to be extremely secure and stable. It also attracted a great deal of interest in academic and industrial research and introduced many new areas of research. Since its launch in 2008, bitcoin has gained popularity and is currently the best performing digital currency in the whole world with billions of dollars invested. It is based on many years of research in the fields of cryptography, digital currency, and distributed computing. The following section presents a brief history that provides the background needed to understand the basics of the invention of bitcoin.

Digital currencies have been an active area of research for decades. The first proposals for making digital money were in the early 80s. In 1982, David Chaum proposed a system that uses a blind signature to create the missing digital currency. In this scheme, the bank would issue digital currency by signing a blind and random serial number that the user would send. The user can use a digital token signed by the bank as currency. The limitation of this scheme was that the bank had to keep track of all the serial numbers used. It was a central system designed by users and their trust. Later, in 1990, David Chaum proposed a sophisticated version called e-cash, which used not only blind signatures but also private identification to write the message, which was then sent to the bank. This system allowed for the detection of double charges but did not avoid them. If the token was used in two different locations, the identity of the double dependent would be revealed. Electronic money can only represent a fixed amount. Adam Backa's hashcash, introduced in 1997, was originally proposed to combat spam. Hashcash aimed to solve a computer puzzle that is easy to verify but relatively difficult to calculate.

The idea was that no additional computing efforts would be noticed for the user and email, but someone who sent a lot of spam would be discouraged because the time and resources needed to run the spam campaign would increase significantly. In 1998, Wei Dai proposed money b, which introduced the idea of using Proof of Work to create money. One of the major weaknesses of the system was that an adversary of higher computing power could generate unwanted money by not allowing the network to adjust to the appropriate level of difficulty. The system does not have details on the consensus mechanism between the nodes and some security issues, and even the Sybil attacks were not resolved. At the exact time, Nick Szabo introduced the concept of BitGold, which was also based on the mechanism of operation but presented the same problems as money b, with the difference that the weight level of the network was adaptable.

Thomas Sander and Ammon TaShama established an electronic ticket system in 1999 that first used Merkle trees to represent coins and zero-knowledge tests to prove possession of coins. In this system, the central bank needed to keep track of all the serial numbers used. This system allowed users to be completely anonymous, but at the expense of computing. RPOW (Repeatable Evidence) was introduced by Hal Finney in 2004 and used the Adam Back hashcash scheme as evidence of the computing resources used to make money.

It was also a central system that maintained a central database to track all prisoners of war. It was an online system that used remote certification thanks to a secure computer platform (TPM material). All of the above-mentioned schemes are cleverly designed, but in one aspect or another, they are weak. All of these systems are constructed on a central server that must be approved by users.

Bitcoin Satoshi Nakamoto wrote a 2008 article on Bitcoin, called *Bitcoin: An Electronic Payment System Between Individuals*. The first key idea introduced in the document was that purely electronic money equally required the intermediary bank transfer between couples. Bitcoin is based on decades of cryptographic research, such as Merkle tree exploration, hash functions, public-key cryptography, and digital signature. In addition, ideas such as BitGold, b-money, hashcash, and the cryptographic timestamp served as the basis for the invention of bitcoin. All of these technologies are cleverly combined in bitcoins to create the world's first decentralized currency. A key problem solved in bitcoin is the elegant solution to the problem of Byzantine generals with a practical solution to the problem of dual consumption.

The regulation of bitcoin is a controversial issue, and whenever it is a libertarian dream, law enforcement agencies and governments propose several regulations to govern it, such as BitLicense published by the Ministry of Services by the State of New York. This is a license issued to companies engaged in activities related to virtual currencies. The growth of Bitcoin is also owing to what is called a network effect. Also called demand-side economics, this is a concept that basically means that the more users use the network, the more valuable it becomes. Over time, the growth of the Bitcoin network has grown exponentially.

Bitcoin definition

Bitcoin can be defined in different ways; It's a protocol, a digital currency, and a platform. It is a combination of peer-to-peer networking, protocols, and software that facilitates the creation and use of digital currency named bitcoin. Note that bitcoin with a capital letter B is used to refer to the bitcoin protocol, while bitcoin with a lowercase b is utilized to refer to bitcoin, the currency. Nodes in this peer-to-peer network interact with each other using the Bitcoin protocol. Currency decentralization was made possible for the first time with the invention of bitcoin. Moreover, the double-spending issue was solved in an elegant and ingenious way in bitcoin. Double spending issue arises when, for example, a user sends coins to two different users at the same time, and they are verified one by one as valid transactions.

Keys and addresses

Elliptic curve cryptography is utilized to generate public and private key pairs in the Bitcoin network. The bitcoin address is developed by taking the corresponding public key of a private key and hashing it two times, initially with the SHA256 algorithm and then with RIPEMD160. The subsequent 160-bit hash is then prefixed with a version number and ultimately encoded with a Base58Check scheme. The bitcoin addresses are 26-35 characters long, and all start with digit 1 or 3.

There are currently two types of addresses, the most commonly used P2PKH, and the other P2SH type, starting with 1 and 3. In their early days, bitcoins used direct payment with a release key, replaced by P2PKH. However, direct payment with a release key is still used in bitcoins for primary addresses. These should not be used more than once; otherwise, privacy and security issues may occur. To avoid reusing addresses, anonymity issues have been omitted to some extent. Bitcoin also creates other security issues, such as transaction corruption, which requires different approaches to solve them.

Public keys in bitcoin

In public-key cryptography, public keys are developed from private keys. Bitcoin uses ECC based on SECP256K1 standard. A random private key is selected, and its length is 256 bits. Public keys can be presented in a compressed or uncompressed format.

The public keys are basically the x and y coordinates in an elliptical curve and in an uncompressed format. They are presented with the prefix 04 in hexadecimal format. The X and Y coordinates are 32 bits long. The compressed public key is 33 bytes long and compares to 65 bytes in an uncompressed format. The compressed version of public keys basically only includes part X, as part of it can be extracted from it. The compressed public key version works because the Bitcoin client initially used uncompressed keys, but from the main Bitcoin client, 0.6 compressed keys are used as standard.

Keys are identified by different prefixes, described as follows:

- Uncompressed public keys u 0x04 as the prefix

- Compressed public key starts with 0x03, when the y 32-bit part of the public key is an odd number

The compressed public key starts at 0x02 if the utilized portion and 32 bits of the public key are even. A more detailed mathematical description and the reason for their action are described here. If an ECC chart is shown, this indicates that the y coordinate may be below the x-axis or over the x-axis; and since the curve is symmetric, only the location of the main field should be registered.

Bitcoin private keys

Private keys are basically 256-bit numbers selected in the range specified in ECDSA SECP256K1. Any random 256-bit number between 0x1 and 0xFFFF. FFFF FFFF FFFF FFFE BBAE DCE6 AF48 A03B BFD2 5E8D D036 4140 is a valid private key. Private keys are generally encrypted using the WIF (Wallet Format Import Format) format for easy copying and use. WIF can be converted to a private key and vice versa. In addition, the form of a mini private key is sometimes used to encode a key of less than 30 characters to allow for storage in tight spaces, such as coin engraving or damage-resistant QR codes. A major bitcoin client also enables wallet encryption containing private keys.

Great Bitcoin Platforms

Getting Your Hands on Hyperledger

Hyperledger is a network of programming engineers and innovation lovers who are building industry guidelines for blockchain systems and platforms. Their work is significant because they're the principal bunch shepherding the blockchain industry into the standard and business selection. Hyperledger is the "sheltered" arrangement stage for enterprise groups. The association and their unique project are developing each day. Now, they have in excess of 100-part organizations and have a few projects in incubation. Their initial few projects include Explorer, a web application to view and question blocks, and Fabric, a fitting and-play blockchain application manufacturer. They additionally have Iroha and Sawtooth, which are modularized blockchain platforms.

Toward the end of 2015, the Linux Foundation shaped the Hyperledger project to build up an enterprise-grade and open-source distributed record structure. They would have liked to concentrate the blockchain network on building strong, industry-explicit applications, platforms, and equipment systems to help businesses. The Linux Foundation saw that there was a wide range of gatherings building blockchain innovation without a durable course. The industry was copying exertion, and the tribalism was driving groups to take care of a similar issue twice. The foundation knew from its encounters that if this innovation was to understand its maximum capacity, an open-source and community-oriented advancement procedure was urgently required.

The Hyperledger project is driven by Executive Director Brian Behlendorf, who has many years of experience going back to the first Linux Foundation and Apache Foundation, just as being a CTO of the World Economic Forum. So, it's not amazing that Hyperledger has been generally welcomed. A significant number of the top business and industry pioneers have joined the project, including Accenture, Cisco, Fujitsu Limited, IBM, J.P. Morgan, Intel, and Wells Fargo. It has likewise pulled in a significant number of the top blockchain organizations. R3, a consortium supporting the financial industry, has contributed its budgetary transaction building structure. Advanced Asset, the product organization, gave the Hyperledger imprint and a portion of its enterprise-grade code. The Factom Foundation is additionally contributing enterprise-grade code and engineer resources. IBM and numerous different organizations are contributing code and different resources to the project.

Hyperledger's specialized guiding advisory groups guarantee vigor and interoperability between these various innovations. The expectation is that the cross-industry, open-source joint effort will progress blockchain innovation and convey billions in monetary incentives by sharing the expenses of innovative work across numerous organizations. Hyperledger is recognizing and addressing the significant highlights and prerequisites missing from the blockchain innovation ecosystem. It's additionally cultivating a cross-industry open standard for distributed records and holding open space for designers to add to building better blockchain systems. Hyperledger has a project life cycle like that of the Linux Foundation. A proposition is submitted, and afterward, the acknowledged recommendations are brought into incubation.

At the point when a project has arrived at a steady-state, it graduates and is moved into a functioning state. Now, all Hyperledger projects are in the proposition or incubation phase. Every one of the projects is led by an enormous organization or startup. For instance, Fabric is led by IBM, Sawtooth by Intel, and Iroha by the startup Soramitsu. Hyperledger, in the same way as other open-source projects, uses GitHub (www.github.com/hyperledger) and Slack (https://slack.hyperledger.org) to associate with groups dealing with every one of the projects. These are incredible spots to get the most recent updates and to check on the advancement that these projects are being developed.

Fabric

Hyperledger's earliest incubation project, Fabric, is a kind of permission blockchain platform. It operates like most blockchains in that it keeps a ledger of computerized instances. These incidents are organized as transactions and shared among the various participants. The transactions are executed without cryptographic money. A discretionary resource for you to jump further into the subject is at https://trustindigitallife.eu/wp-

content/transfers/2016/07/marko_vukolic.pdf. All transactions are verified, private, and classified. Fabric must be refreshed by the consensus of the participants. At the point when records have been inputted, they can never be modified.

Fabric is an enterprise arrangement intrigued by adaptability and being in consistence with guidelines. All participants must enroll evidence of character to participation benefits so as to access the system. Fabric issues transactions with inferred declarations that are unlinkable to the owning participant; in this manner, offering secrecy on the network. Likewise, the content of every transaction is scrambled to guarantee just the intended participants can see the content. Fabric has a secluded architecture.

You can include or take route parts by actualizing its convention particular. Its compartment innovation can deal with a large portion of the standard languages for smart contracts advancement. Bitcoin, then again, enables anybody to take an interest secretly, and the network is continually searching for approaches to be restriction safe and to empower the individuals who have been disappointed. Bitcoin was additionally, for the most part, built for the development and security of its cryptographic money token. Therefore, contrasting the prescribed procedures of Bitcoin with those of Fabric might be unreasonable.

Building your system in Fabric

A lot of work has been carried out to make Fabric available, but only accessible to people with technical knowledge. Hyperledger detailed several use cases for which he simply directs his technology. You can use Fabric in future use cases with intuitive user interfaces. For now, you can develop and test use cases listed with the help of a leading developer.

Diving into Chaincode Development

Contracts between two parties can be converted into code on the Hyperledger Fabric through Chaincode. Chaincode is Hyperledger's rendition of Ethereum's smart contract. It mechanizes the understandings made inside a contract such that the two parties can trust. Chaincode is Turing finished like the smart contracts of Ethereum. As of now, you can have a Java engineer construct a chaincode contract for you. The Fabric team has arranged some regular use cases, for example, advanced monetary forms and sending instant messages as a major aspect of the central system. The Fabric team is additionally investigating other intriguing business use cases that were not finished at the time of this composition yet might be accessible when you're understanding this. Hyperledger is right off the bat being developed, and its projects are around two years behind Ethereum's work. Notwithstanding, every one of the projects has considerable teams and resources committed to it.

Business contracts

Hyperledger has thought of approaches to have both public contracts and private contracts. Private contracts are between at least two parties and contain secret data. Public contracts are distinguishable by any individual who sets aside the effort to look for them inside Hyperledger. For instance, you may use a public contract to make a public idea to sell an item or as an approach to request offers on a contract. The cosmetics of these contracts are more complex than customary contracts because intervention and outsider authorization are expelled. Furthermore, the confirmation of the people partaking in the contract is required. Also, most contracts are unique and can't be institutionalized. The more sophisticated the contract, the more places it very well may be defiled from its unique plan. Hyperledger is dealing with making a contract with the executives' system to help upgrade the versatility of Chaincode.

Contracts between two parties can be converted into code on the Hyperledger Fabric by means of Chaincode. Chaincode is Hyperledger's variant of Ethereum's smart contract. It computerizes the understandings made inside a contract such that the two parties can trust. Chaincode is Turing finished like the smart contracts of Ethereum. As of now, you can have a Java engineer construct a chaincode contract for you. The Fabric team has arranged some basic use cases, for example, computerized monetary standards and sending instant messages as a feature of the central system. The Fabric team is likewise investigating other fascinating business use cases that were not finished at the time of this composition, however, might be accessible when you're understanding this. Hyperledger is right off the bat being developed, and its projects are around two years behind Ethereum's work. However, every one of the projects has considerable teams and resources dedicated to it.

Business contracts

Hyperledger has thought of approaches to have both public contracts and private contracts. Private contracts are between at least two parties and contain classified data. Public contracts are distinguishable by any individual who sets aside the effort to look for them inside Hyperledger. For instance, you may use a public contract to make a public idea to sell an item or as an approach to request offers on a contract. The cosmetics of these contracts are more complex than conventional contracts because mediation and outsider implementation are expelled. Furthermore, the confirmation of the people taking an interest in the contract is required. Additionally, most contracts are unique and can't be institutionalized. The more complicated the contract, the more places it tends to be debased from its unique goal. Hyperledger is chipping away at making a contract with the executives' system to help upgrade the adaptability of Chaincode.

Manufacturing supply chain

Supply is an empowering blockchain contrive that is being researched on Fabric. Last developing specialists could manage all the fragment parts and supplies that they used in making their products. This section would enable you to be responsive to feedback and have the choice to pursue back the wellspring of each part to the primary producer. Because of a product survey, it is definitely not hard to find the blameworthy party or the capacity to tell the realness of each part before it's used. Fabric requires more noteworthy progression before it's set up for this use case because it ought to be adequately accessible to everyone in the supply chain. The Fabric team is wearing down a standard convention to allow every participant on a supply chain network to enter and to pursue numbered parts that are conveyed and used on a particular product. Exactly when it's set, this use case would empower significant missions to be done on the production of each product at whatever point. This might be, at any rate, ten layers someplace down in the production of anything. Consumers could then set up the provenance of any delivered benefit that is included in other part products and supplies. This may have a captivating social impact on use.

Securities and assets

Securities and various assets are suitable to blockchain because they can motorize a critical number of the functions that outsiders perform. Fabric will empower all partners of an asset to have direct access to that asset and its beautifying agents and history, bypassing intermediaries that by and by holds that data. Fabric will likewise quicken the settlement time on assets to approach real-time.

Direct communication

In the future, Fabric could likewise be used as a spot where companies can make public announcements and offers. For instance, if an association needed to raise assets and expected to instruct all shareholders with respect to the complete nuances of the idea in real time, it could. Like the decentralized self-administering affiliation (DAO) of Ethereum, shareholders can choose choices and execute them. Their choices will be processed and settled in real time. This will make speculator get-togethers and throwing a voting form significantly more straightforward and speedier.

Interoperability of assets: In the coming, Fabric may likewise have a bit of a comparative functionality as the Ripple network. It has imagined use cases where startups could exchange assets low-liquidity publicizes by organizing demands between various parties. As opposed to making do with showcase limits on direct trading between two parties, a chain network interfaces buyers with shippers and finds the best match across various asset classes. Hyperledger is by all accounts, especially arranged in the future to trade subsidiaries.

Investigating the Iroha Project

Hyperledger's Iroha project is expanding on the work finished in the Fabric project. It's intended to supplement Fabric, Sawtooth Lake, and different projects under Hyperledger. Hyperledger included the Iroha project to incubation because different projects didn't have any foundation projects written in C++. Not having a C++ project seriously constrained what number of people could profit from the work on Hyperledger and the number of designers who could add to the project. What's more, most blockchain advancement now has been at the least foundation level, and there has been practically zero improvement deal with user association or portable applications. Hyperledger accepts that Iroha is vital for the promotion of blockchain innovation. This project fills the hole in the market by getting more engineers and giving libraries to portable user interface improvement. No, Iroha is another project and has not coordinated with Fabric or Sawtooth Lake. Hyperledger has plans to grow functionality to work with the other blockchain projects soon. Its iOS, Android, and JavaScript libraries will give steady functions like carefully marking transactions. It will be extremely useful for business application advancement, and it will include new layers of security and business models just conceivable with blockchain innovation.

Applying Microsoft Azure

This section helps you compete, collaborate, and serve clients in the global economy. Blockchain technology is opening up new markets and changing business models. Microsoft is working hard to make it a valuable technology for traditional businesses. This section also explains innovative bridges designed to enable existing systems to connect and evolve. You will learn how to implement your own blockchain in Azure and discover the keys to creating a secure and smooth transition to blockchain systems for your business.

Bletchley: The Modular Blockchain Fabric Project

Bletchley focuses on providing architectural building blocks for client companies within the blockchain consortium ecosystem (member-only networks authorized by members to execute contracts). The Bletchley Fabric blockchain platform is powered by Azure, a cloud computing platform for Microsoft. The Bletchley project addresses the following points:

- Digital identity

- Private key management

- Customer privacy

- Data security

- Operations administration

- System interoperability

At Project Bletchley, Azure provides a cloud layer for the blockchain, which serves as a platform for application creation and delivery. It will be available in 24 regions of the world. Azure combines traditional products, such as hybrid cloud features, full compliance with portfolio certification, and enterprise-level security with several blockchains. Microsoft wants to facilitate the rapid adoption of blockchain technology by existing customers, especially in controlled sectors such as healthcare, financial services, and government.

Azure will work with several blockchain protocols. They are part of the Hyperledger project and protocols based on the outcome of unused transactions (UTXO). This means that the Azure platform will use cryptocurrencies and may be more attractive to businesses. They also have integrations with more sophisticated protocols, including Ethereum, which use cryptocurrencies to protect the network.

Cryptlets for Encrypting and Authenticating

Project Bletchley is built around two ideas which are:

Blockchain middleware: Identity management, analytics, cloud storage, and machine learning.

Cryptlets: Secure execution for communication and interoperation between Microsoft Azure, Bletchley's ecosystem, and your own technology.

Cryptlets are built as off-chaincode elements, written in any language, executed within a trusted container, and communicated over a secure channel. Cryptlets can be used in UTXO systems and smart contracts when additional functionality or information is needed. Cryptlets close the gap in security between on-and off-chain execution of programs, operating when additional security information is needed. They're what allows your customer relationship management (CRM) or trading platform to connect with your cloud storage and then be protected with Ethereum, for example. Bletchley's middleware performs in tandem with Cryptlets and existing Azure services, like Active Directory and Key Vault, and other technologies of blockchains' ecosystems, to deliver a complete solution and ensure the reliable operation of your blockchain integration.

Building in the Azure Ecosystem

Azure is a digital ecosystem and platform for cloud computing. Connect businesses directly with their cloud and SaaS partners. This allows companies to transfer their information in an interconnected, reliable, and secure manner. Microsoft's Azure cloud platform is the second largest infrastructure as a service (IaaS) platform. It is a reliable and secure haven for cloud computing and data storage. In Azure, there is a service called ExpressRoute that offers consumers a way to connect directly to Azure. This avoids work and safety issues that are widely available on the public internet.

In 2015, Microsoft resolved to expand its Azure ecosystem using Ethereum and Hyperledger chain locks. Azure Blockchain's first offering as a service is run by Ethereum. Ethereum is a complete Turing blockchain framework for construction applications. Microsoft aims to create more blockchain and Hyperledger technology offerings. It also develops the Azure market when it makes the transition to the Azure customer portal. Microsoft's Azure Stack software includes templates for Azure QuickStart that implement various Azure resources with the help of Azure Resource Manager to help you get more done. Azure Resource Manager allows customers to work with their business resources as a group. This allows them to coordinate the implementation, removal, or update of all resources in their solution.

The Azure Quickstart models can work in many environments, such as production, staging, and testing. With Azure Resource Manager, customers have multiple tagging, auditing, and security features. These features help consumers manage their resources after use. Microsoft Bletchley Project is its blockchain architecture that integrates with the established business technologies they have already offered. This provides Azure with support and a blockchain market. The Bletchley ecosystem is an approach taken by Microsoft to provide blockbuster or distributed blockchain networks to a wider audience in an efficient and safe manner. They want to help develop authentic solutions and solve real business problems.

Getting Started with Chain on Azure

Chain, which offers blockchain technology solutions, has launched its Chain Core Developer Edition program in Azure. Chain Core Developer Edition is a free, open-source version of the company's distributed accounting platform. It allows you to issue and transfer assets on authorized blockchain networks. Through the test network, its developers can join or run a blockchain, access detailed technical guides and documentation, and create financial applications. They can also run their own prototypes in the test chain or create their own personal network in Azure.

Chain has launched its free and open-source development platform. It includes a test network, managed by Microsoft, Chain, and the Cryptocurrency and Contracts Initiative (3CI). 3CI is a Chain-launched platform that provides blockchain technology solutions. This is a release for Chain Core developers. This platform enables the issue and transfer of assets on authenticated blockchain networks. Chain. Several financial applications can be developed through Chain Core. Many new and innovative products must be launched on this platform. The range covers payments, banking, insurance, and the capital market. In addition, Visa has partnered with Chain to develop a secure, fast, and easy way to process B2B payments worldwide.

DECENTRALIZATION

Decentralization is not a new concept. It has long been used in the areas of strategy, management, and governance. The basic idea of decentralization is to extend control and authority over the periphery, rather than giving one central body complete control over the organization. This means several benefits for organizations, such as greater efficiency, faster decision-making, better motivation, and less administrative burden. In this section, the concept of decentralization will be addressed in the context of the blockchain; The goals of the two are similar, with no central authority in control. Decentralization and decentralization modes will also be presented with some examples. Blockchain ecosystem decentralization, decentralized applications, and decentralization platforms will be further discussed.

Decentralization using blockchain

Decentralization is a fundamental advantage and service provided by blockchain technology. Blockchain is by design the ideal vehicle to provide a platform that requires no intermediaries and can work with many different leaders selected through consensual mechanisms. This model allows anyone to compete and becomes a decision-making authority. This contest is governed by a consensus mechanism, and the most commonly used method is known as "proof of work."

Decentralization is implemented to varying degrees, from semi-decentralized to fully decentralized, according to needs and circumstances. Decentralization can be seen from a blockchain perspective as a mechanism to modify existing applications and paradigms or create new applications for complete control of users. Information and communication technologies (ICTs) are generally based on a centralized paradigm according to which databases or application servers are controlled by a central authority, such as a system administrator. With Bitcoin and the introduction of blockchain technology, this model has changed, and technology is available that allows anyone to run a decentralized system (and allow it to operate without any failure or reliable authorization). It can run on its own or require human intervention, depending on the type and model of government used in a decentralized application running in the blockchain.

Centralized systems are traditional computer systems (client-server) in which one body controls the system and is solely responsible for all system operations. All central system users depend on one source of service. Internet service providers, such as eBay, Google, Amazon, the Apple App Store, and most other providers, use this common service model. In a distributed system, contrarily, data, and budgets are distributed across several nodes in the network. Sometimes this term is mixed up with parallel computing. Although the definition overlaps, the main difference between the two systems lies in the fact that in a parallel system, all nodes perform the calculation simultaneously to obtain a result, whereas in a distributed system, the calculation cannot be made in parallel and data is replicated only to multiple nodes that users consider to be a unique and consistent system. Both models are used with variations to achieve tolerance and error rate. In this model, there is always a central body that controls all nodes and controls processing. This means that the system is always centralized.

The main difference between a decentralized system and a distributed system is that in a distributed system, there is always a central body managing the whole system, while in a decentralized system, there is no such authority. There a decentralized system is a kind of network in which nodes are not dependent on either one main node; it is possible, the control is distributed among several nodes. For example, this is an analog model in which each company department has its own database server, which pulls it from a source and distributes it to sub-services that manage its own data. The decentralized consensus, introduced with bitcoin, is the real innovation or decentralization of paradigms at the beginning of this new decentralization application. To take full advantage of the ability to submit something through a consensus algorithm, without the need for trusted third parties, intermediation or reliable service provider.

Methods of decentralization

There are two methods that can be utilized to achieve decentralization. These methods are talked about in detail in the following sections.

Disintermediation

This can be explained by an example. Imagine wanting to send money to a friend in another country. You will go to a bank that will transfer money to a bank of your choice for a fee. In this case, the bank maintains an updated central database confirming that it has sent the money. With blockchain technology, you can send money directly to your friend without the need for a bank. All you need is your blockchain friend's address. In this way, the mediator is no longer needed, and decentralization achieves disintermediation. However, it is questionable to what extent decentralization is tangible in the financial sector due to the disruption of mediation due to regulatory and harmonized requirements. However, this model can be used not only in finance but in many other industries.

Through competition

A group of service providers competes to select the services to be provided by the system in this method. This paradigm does not allow for complete decentralization, but to some extent, guarantees that the intermediary or service provider does not monopolize the service. In the frame of reference of blockchain technology, a system can be envisioned in which smart contracts can choose a third-party data provider from a large number of providers based on their reputation, past performance, ratings, and quality. This will not result in complete decentralization, but it will allow smart contracts to make a free decision based on the above criteria. This way, service providers maintain a competitive bidding climate to become the data providers of their choice.

Scale of decentralization

While there are many advantages of decentralization--including but not limited to transparency, efficiency, cost-saving, development of trusted ecosystems, and in certain cases privacy and anonymity, some challenges, such as security requirements, software bugs, and human errors, also require to be looked at thoroughly. For instance, in a decentralized system such as bitcoin or Ethereum, in which security is typically secured by private keys, how can it be ensured that a smart property linked with these private keys cannot be made irrelevant due to a human error? Say the private keys are lost, owing to a bug in the smart contract code, the decentralized application is vulnerable to attack by hackers. Before we kick-off on a journey to decentralize everything using blockchain and decentralized applications, it is important to comprehend that not everything is required to (or can be) decentralized.

Routes to decentralization

Even though a few systems existed before bitcoin or blockchain that can be classed as decentralized in a specific way, for example, BitTorrent or Gnutella file sharing, with the approach of the blockchain technology, numerous activities are being taken all together to leverage this new technology for decentralization.

Ordinarily, the bitcoin blockchain remains the best choice for some as it has demonstrated to be the strongest and secure blockchain with a market cap of very nearly 12 billion dollars. An alternative approach is to use different blockchains, for example, Ethereum, which is, as of now, the apparatus of choice of numerous developers for building decentralized applications.

Storage

Data can be stored straightforwardly in a blockchain, and with this, it achieves decentralization, yet a significant detriment of this approach is that blockchain isn't suitable for putting away a lot of data by plan. It can store straightforward transactions, and some self-assertive data, however, is positively not suitable for putting away pictures or huge masses of data, similar to the case in customary database systems. A superior alternative is to use distributed hash tables (DHTs). DHTs were initially used in peer-to-peer file sharing programming, for example, BitTorrent, Napster, Kazaa, and Gnutella. DHT research was made prevalent by CAN, Chord, Pastry, and Tapestry projects. BitTorrent ends up being the most scalable and quick network, yet the issue is that there is no encouragement for users to keep the files inconclusively. Users don't, as a rule, keep files for all time, and if nodes leave the network that has data required by somebody, there is no real way to recover it aside from having the necessary nodes rejoin the network again with the goal that the files become accessible again. Two fundamental prerequisites here are high accessibility and link stability, which implies that data ought to be accessible when required, and network links ought to likewise consistently be accessible. Entomb Planetary File System (IPFS) by Juan Benet has both of these properties, and the vision is to produce a decentralized World Wide Web by supplanting the HTTP protocol. IPFS uses Kademlia DHT and Merkle DAG (Directed Acyclic Graph) to provide storage and functionality, separately.

The incentive mechanism depends on a protocol known as Filecoin that pays incentives to nodes that store data utilizing the BitSwap mechanism. The BitSwap mechanism enables nodes to keep a basic ledger of bytes sent, or bytes got under a balanced relationship. Likewise, a Git-based rendition control mechanism is used in IPFS to provide structure and command over the forming of data. There are different alternatives, for example, Ethereum swarm, storj, and maidsafe. Ethereum has its very own decentralized and distributed ecosystem that uses Swarm for storage and the whisper protocol for communication. Maidsafe is expecting to provide a decentralized World Wide Web. Every one of these projects will be talked about later in the book in more detail. BigChainDB is another storage layer decentralization project planned for giving a scalable, quick, and directly scalable decentralized database instead of a customary filesystem. BigChainDB supplements decentralized processing platforms and file systems, for example, Ethereum and IPFS.

Communication

It is generally thought that the Internet (the communication layer in the blockchain) is decentralized. This is applicable to some extent as the original vision of the Internet was to develop a decentralized system. Services such as online storage and e-mail are all now based on a paradigm where the service provider is in power, and users trust them to give them access to Service as needed. This model is based on the trust of the central body (service providers), and users do not control their data; Even passwords are stored in trusted third-party systems. It is necessary to provide control to individual users so that access to their data is guaranteed and does not depend on a third party. Internet access (communication layer) is based on Internet Service Providers (ISPs), which act as a central hub for Internet users. If the ISP is closed for political reasons or for any other reason, communication in this model is not possible. An alternative is to use mesh nets. Although they have limited functionality over the Internet, they still offer a decentralized alternative where nodes can communicate directly with each other without a central hub, such as an ISP.

Computation

Decentralization of computing or processing is achieved by blockchain technology like Ethereum, where smart contracts with integrated business logic can be executed online. Other blockchain technologies also provide similar platforms for processing layers where business logic can be decentralized online.

For the decentralized ecosystem, the bottom layer Internet or

Meshnets provides a decentralized communication layer, then the storage layer uses technologies such as IPFS and BigChainDB to enable decentralization, and finally sees a blockchain that serves as a layer for decentralized processing. Blockchain may also provide a storage layer in a limited way, but this seriously impedes the speed and capacity of the system; hence, other solutions such as IPFS and BigChainDB are more suitable for storing substantial amounts of data in a decentralized manner. The top shows layers of identity and wealth. Internet identity is a very important issue, and systems like bitAuth and OpenID have authentication and authentication services with varying degrees of decentralization and security assumptions.

Blockchain Disruption

Blockchain technology and cryptocurrencies like Bitcoin have generated a lot of news this year. Every week, it seems like a different title is promoting a revolution or minimizing this new technology as a fashion with some long-term perspectives. If you are not familiar with blockchain technology or are always building your position, let me advocate a revolution.

Recipe for harassment.

Let's start with why we believe we do business with a company. We are confident that our largest retailers will make purchases to deliver goods and services. We rely on our banks to ensure that our account balance is correct and that transfers are verified and fraud-free. The systems implemented by these companies strengthen our confidence. For example, anti-fraud regulations, systems, and services play an important role in business security and are pushed to the limit. Credit card companies are a specific example of a third party that charges a fee each time they make a purchase to confirm and make a loan to the consumer. Generally, each of these parties acts as an intermediary and provides remuneration services in each transaction.

The volume of transactions in our global economy is incredible. Worldwide retail sales are over US $ 20 billion each year, with the global gross product (PCG) exceeding US $ 100 billion. This is a large number of transactions that use intermediaries and their audit services to manage trusted companies. As a business expense, we accept that these brokers are drawing fees in billions of transactions to curb fraud and maintain consumer confidence. These costs infiltrate the economy, increasing the cost of living and the prices of goods and services.

But what if there are cheaper or faster ways to verify transactions in our economy? If there were alternatives, the savings would be $ 1 billion. For example, online payment gateways earn billions by adding more than 2.9% in each transaction. There is also the cost of lost time. All brokers add mortgage days and weeks, loan approval, or license renewal. Reducing the cost of every transaction and order in the economy would mean making incredible profits for businesses and ending the way they do business. Making billions of dollars in savings would drive the growth of the global economy more than any government or company alone could.

In comes the blockchain

Blockchain technology is basically a decentralized system for recording trusted transactions without intermediaries. Thanks to cryptographic power, each transaction is irreversibly linked and shared on a computer network. Network computers automatically check the terms of transactions, acting as instant counters by "checking books" at no cost. Automatic transaction verification is a core feature of blockchain technology.

That's how cryptocurrencies like Bitcoin work. There are a limited number of pieces obtained when solving computer puzzles or purchasing them from another person. Someone with a puzzle solution can check ownership of their piece because their test is registered in the blockchain below. Network participants cryptographically verify the identity and integrity of the evidence of others to ensure who owns the parts.

The effect of the blockchain concept is clear. By using blockchain technology, companies could save billions of dollars and deliver services faster. More specifically, they could:

- Eliminating transaction testing costs is a legitimate third-party service that saves billions of dollars a year.

- Provide faster service by instantly checking the terms of the transaction, eliminating indirect services such as banks, governments, and markets.

- Deliver more securely, using security built into the blockchain without any additional investment.

- Automate more complex businesses, such as insurance services, with scheduled smart contracts.

BLOCKCHAIN AND FULL ECOSYSTEM DECENTRALIZATION

In order to reach total decentralization, it is necessary that the environment around the blockchain is also decentralized. Blockchain itself is a distributed record that runs on top of conventional systems. These elements include communication, storage, and computation. There are other factors, such as Identity and Wealth, that are conventionally based on centralized paradigms; there's a need to decentralize these aspects too in order to achieve a fully decentralized ecosystem.

Storage

Data can be put away directly in a blockchain, and with this, it achieves decentralization; however, a significant impediment of this methodology is that blockchain isn't suitable for putting away a lot of data by plan. It can store basic exchanges and some subjective data, though, it is positively not suitable for putting away pictures or huge masses of data, just like the case in conventional database frameworks. A superior option is to utilize disseminated hash tables (DHTs). DHTs were initially utilized in distributed document sharing programming, for example, BitTorrent, Napster, Kazaa, and Gnutella. DHT explore was made famous by CAN, Chord, Pastry, and Tapestry ventures. BitTorrent ends up being the most scalable and quick network; however, the issue is that there is no motivation for users to keep the records inconclusively. Users don't, for the most part, keep records for all time, and if nodes leave the network that has data required by somebody, there is no real way to recover it with the exception of having the necessary nodes rejoin the network again, so the documents become accessible again. Two fundamental necessities here are high accessibility and connection steadiness, which implies that data ought to be accessible when required, and network connections ought to likewise consistently be available. Bury Planetary File System (IPFS) by Juan Benet has both of these properties, and the vision is to provide a decentralized World Wide Web by supplanting the HTTP convention.

IPFS utilizes Kademlia DHT and Merkle DAG (Directed Acyclic Graph) to provide the storage and looking through usefulness, separately. The impetus mechanism depends on a convention known as Filecoin that pays motivators to nodes that store data utilizing the BitSwap mechanism. The BitSwap mechanism enables nodes to keep a straightforward record of bytes sent, or bytes got under a coordinated relationship. Additionally, a Git-based variant control mechanism is utilized in IPFS to provide structure and power over the forming of data. There are different other options, for example, Ethereum swarm, storj, and maidsafe. Ethereum has its very own decentralized and dispersed biological system that utilizations Swarm for storage and the murmur convention for correspondence. Maidsafe intends to provide a decentralized World Wide Web. Every one of these activities will be talked about later in the book in more detail. BigChainDB is another storage layer decentralization venture planned for giving a scalable, quick, and directly scalable decentralized database rather than a conventional filesystem. BigChainDB supplements decentralized handling stages and record frameworks, for example, Ethereum and IPFS.

Communication

Generally, the Internet (communication layer in the blockchain) is considered decentralized. This is true to some extent because the original vision of the Internet was to develop a decentralized system. Services such as email and electronic storage are now based on a paradigm in which the service provider has control, and users rely on them to allow them access to the service when needed. This model is based on the trust of the central body (service providers), and users do not control their data; even passwords are stored in trusted third-party systems. Individual users need to be monitored to ensure that their data is accessed rather than relying on a third party. Internet access (communication layer) is based on Internet Service Providers (ISPs), which act as a central hub for Internet users. If the ISP is closed for political reasons or for any other reason, communication in this model is not possible. An alternative is to use mesh nets. Although they have limited functionality over the Internet, they still offer decentralized alternatives where nodes can communicate directly with each other without a central hub, such as an ISP.

Computation

Decentralization of computing or processing is accomplished by a blockchain innovation, for example, Ethereum, where savvy contracts with installed business rationale can run on the network. Other blockchain innovations additionally provide comparative processing layer platforms where business rationale can run over the network in a decentralized way. The following outline shows the decentralized ecosystem diagram where, on the base layer, the Internet or Meshnets provides a decentralized correspondence layer; at that point, a storage layer utilizes innovations, for example, IPFS and BigChainDB to empower decentralization. Lastly, you see the blockchain that fills in as a decentralized processing layer. Blockchain can, in a restricted way, provide a storage layer as well, yet that genuinely hampers the speed and limit of the system; therefore, different arrangements, for example, IPFS and BigChainDB, are more suitable to store a lot of data in a decentralized manner.

At the top, the identity and wealth layers appear. Identity on the Internet is an extremely large theme and system. For example, bitAuth and OpenID have provided confirmation and distinguishing proof administrations with differing degrees of decentralization and security presumptions. Blockchain is fit for giving answers to different issues. An idea significant to Identity known as Zooko's Triangle necessitates that a naming system in a network convention secure, decentralized, and important to people. It is guessed that a system can have just two of these properties all the while, yet with the coming of blockchain, as Namecoin, this issue was settled. This, so, isn't a panacea and accompanies its own difficulties, for example, dependence on users to store and maintain private keys safely. This opens up other general inquiries regarding the appropriateness of decentralization. Maybe decentralization isn't suitable in each situation. Well-reputed unified systems will, in general, work better by and large.

SMART CONTRACTS

A smart contract is a computer protocol intended to carefully facilitate, check, or implement the arrangement or performance of a contract. Smart contracts permit the performance of solid transactions without outsiders. Probably the best thing about the blockchain is that, because it is a decentralized system that exists between all allowed parties, there's no need to pay intermediaries (Middlemen), and it spares you time and strife. Blockchains have their issues; that being said, they are valued, they're quicker, less expensive, and more secure than customary systems, which is the reason banks and governments are going to them.

Blockchain technology is known for electronic installments, yet there are a lot more uses. With smart contracts, anything can be enlisted carefully, as for example "birth and death certificates, marriage licenses, deeds and titles of ownership, instructive degrees, money related records, restorative procedures, protection claims, cast a ballot, provenance of nourishment." Smart contracts run on the blockchain and subsequently have similar characteristics, for example, transparency and cryptography. A smart contract can be considered as a contract that is programmed in a computer code. At least two parties carefully concur upon specific rights, commitments, and potential outcomes. The contract is "recorded in the blockchain and executed by distributed nodes of the network, which dispenses with the need for a confided in an outsider." The contract will execute itself and will act precisely as coded. This empowers an expansive variety of uses: a programmed installment dependent on a wager, paying and opening entryways for an Airbnb house, discharging money related aid after a specific time of escrow, giving protection installments after requirements are consequently checked, sending installments if someone prevails in a web-based adapting course, etc.

In any case, the term smart contract can be misleading. The term is neither smart nor essentially a contract. The contract is a computer code, which for the prevalent smart contract platform Ethereum, is written in the JavaScript-like language Solidity. The blockchain executes the contract precisely, as indicated by what was programmed. This suggests every single imaginable result ought to be resolved beforehand. The smart contract essentially does what it is programmed to do and doesn't play out any master action. Smart contracts likewise don't need to be considered contracts as they are not properly official.

The smart contract can be invoked by internal entities (other smart contracts) and external (external data sources) of the blockchain. Among these entities, the so-called "orcs" insert relevant information for the smart world contract into the smart contract information bank. If properly implemented, smart contracts could offer transaction security over traditional contract law, reducing the cost of coordinating the audit and implementation of those agreements. They can monitor the effect of the agreement in real time and can reduce costs as compliance and control are on the move. Smart contracts reduce the cost of contract transactions by order sizes; in particular, they reduce the cost of (I) contracting, (II) formalization, and (III) enforcement. Smart contracts also avoid the so-called dilemma of the organization's principal agent, providing more transparency and accountability and less red tape.

With smart contracts, each agreement, each process, undertaking, and installment can have an advanced record and mark that could be identified, validated, stored, and shared. Time-stamping services like "Bernstein" (patent vault), or legislative and semi-administrative libraries (land titles, birth testaments, school, and college degrees), are examples for straightforward technological use cases. While time-stamping services are easy to actualize on a specialized level, the administrative parts of such use cases may be considerably more complex, depending on the sort of industry and explicit use-case. Smart contracts can besides be used for significantly more complex understandings between a large number of on-screen characters, along the supply chain of merchandise or services, or for administering a gathering of people that offer similar interests and objectives without the need for conventional centralized establishments. Decentralized Autonomous Organizations (DAOs) are such an example and likely speak to the most complex smart contracts. The smart contract thusly formalizes the administration rules – the bylaws, overseeing resolutions, rules of technique, or articles of the relationship of an association – and replaces everyday operational management with a self-authorizing code.

Smart contracts have been considered potentially progressive across a range of ventures, with certain observers going to the extent of colloquialism that they will supplant customary contracts and lawyers. The individuals who state smart contracts will render lawyers useless typically accept the whole legitimate understanding is communicated in its code. Basically implying that code is law and accordingly lawyers are probably not going to be required – except if they are additionally designers. All in all, smart contracts are seen to be code (not law) used to mechanize the execution of a hidden lawful understanding.

Oracles

Many smart contracts can be dependent on outside values. For example, the result of a football coordinate in a wagering contract. Smart contracts utilize a purported oracle to gather data. The oracle is a source that provides contribution for the smart contract. With the football wager example, an oracle could be the universal football association that distributed the match results on their site. A downside to utilizing an oracle is that an outsider goes about as a delegate, which is conflicting to the standards of blockchain that no outsider is needed.

Example of a Smart Contract

Assume you lease an apartment from me. You can perform this through the blockchain by paying in cryptographic money. You get a receipt which is kept in our virtual contract; I give you the advanced passage key which comes to you by a predefined date. If the key doesn't come on time, the blockchain discharges a discount. In the event that I send the key before the rental date, the function holds it, discharging both the expense and key to you and me separately when the date shows up. The system takes a shot at the If-Then reason and is witnessed by several people, so you can anticipate a perfect conveyance. If I give you the key, I'm certain to be paid. If you send a specific sum in bitcoins, you get the key. The document is consequently canceled after some time, and the code can't be tampered with by any of us without the other knowing since all participants are all the while cautioned. You can use smart contracts for all sorts of circumstances that range from budgetary subsidiaries to protection premiums, rupture contracts, property law, credit implementation, monetary services, legitimate processes, and crowdfunding understandings.

How You Can Use Smart Contracts

Government

Insiders vouch that it is incredibly hard for our democratic system to be fixed, yet in any case, smart contracts would alleviate all worries by providing an interminably increasingly secure system. Ledger-ensured votes would need to be decoded and require unreasonable figuring capacity to access. Nobody has that much registering force, so it would need God to hack the system! Also, smart contracts could climb low voter turnout. A great part of the inactivity originates from a bungling system that incorporates arranging, demonstrating your identity, and finishing forms. With smart contracts, volunteers can transfer casting a ballot on the web, and 20 to 30-year-olds will turn out to decide in favor of their Potus.

Management

The blockchain not just provides a solitary ledger as a wellspring of trust, yet additionally shaves potential growls in communication and work process because of its precision, transparency, and mechanized system. Normally, business tasks need to endure a to and fro, while sitting tight for approvals and for inner or outside issues to sort themselves out. A blockchain ledger streamlines this. It likewise removes inconsistencies that commonly happen with independent processing, and that may prompt expensive lawsuits and settlement delays.

Examination with customary contracts

Traditional contracts

The term smart contracts suggest an association with customary contracts. As indicated by the Oxford word reference, the definition of a contract is: "A composed or spoken understanding, particularly one concerning work, deals, or occupancy, that is intended to be enforceable by law." The definition of when something is an understanding contrasts for each nation. For example, the Dutch law expresses that an understanding is valid when two criteria are met: there is an offer of one party, and every single included party acknowledges the offer. These definitions don't reject advanced understandings and smart contracts, as they are carefully composed and host the gatherings concur upon offered terms. The US law further indicates a contract with four criteria a contract ought to have:

1. Offer – One party offers some predefined terms;

2. Consideration – Something significant is guaranteed in return for assistance, product or activity;

3. Acknowledgment – The other party acknowledges the offer;

4. Commonality – Both parties comprehend the terms and commonly concur upon it.

Issues with smart contracts

A smart contract is only a specific application of blockchain technology, with certain characteristics that are different from other blockchain applications. Therefore some issues that are observed are specific for smart contracts. This section looks at issues that are specifically occurring with smart contracts.

Legal inflexibility and uncertainty

The term smart contract implies a legal relationship between parties. The smart contract is automatically executed and becomes irrevocable once the contract is deployed on the blockchain. If, however, one of the parties cannot comply with one or more of the conditions, there is a lack of flexibility to deal with this. In contract law, lawyers have the freedom to interpret the contract and handle unforeseen situations. With smart contracts, this is not possible. There is no third party that can change conditions, and thus all possible outcomes should be accounted for in advance. This restricts smart contracts to handle only simple situations with clear rules, variables, and outcomes.

Also, the legal status of smart contracts is unclear. When a smart contract specifies that someone needs to perform a physical act, it is not possible for the smart contract to verify this. If, for example, someone will be paid €100 to give a performance, the smart contract code cannot verify this physical act. In traditional contract law, the contract will be enforced by a third party. This party will acknowledge the legal status of the contract and demands the parties of the contract to comply. With a smart contract, however, there is no third party to enforce it. As a matter of fact, the main motive of smart contracts is to avoid the necessity of a third party. It is possible to give the smart contracts a legal status, after which it is possible to enforce them through traditional authorities. However, until national laws for smart contracts are drafted, their status remains unclear.

Technical issues

Due to the technical nature of smart contracts, several technical issues arise. These are the same technical issues as blockchain in general, but some are specific for smart contracts. One of them is known as the code is law-discussion. This is best explained by the example of the DAO-hack. In this massive attack, a small vulnerability allowed a hacker to receive approximately $60 million value of cryptocurrencies. The DAO was a fundraising platform that used smart contracts. The hacker used the vulnerability in such a way that it seemed that individuals only made one payment, while they actually sent their entire balance. The interesting part was that the smart contract was executed perfectly well. It was the application of DAO that had the vulnerability. The solution was a hard fork. That would split the blockchain in such a way that it was agreed to start over from a block before the hack, and the blocks with transactions from the hack were simply not supported anymore.

Lack of best practices

Though the principles of smart contracts were already described 20 years ago by Nick Szabo, the first smart contract powered platform was only just proposed and developed in 2013. Applications that use smart contracts, like the smart lock start-up Slock.it, have been developed in the last few years, but the field is still new. Hence, there is still much unclarity in the approach to smart contracts, and only a few policy recommendations have been made. Mass adoption of smart contracts is, however, hindered by amongst others' privacy concerns and the difficulty of understanding the fundamentals that are underlying smart contracts. Capgemini argues that mass adoption will only begin to start somewhere after 2020. The lack of real life use cases, experience from applications, and mass adoption are causes for lack of best practices. Without best practices, new applications start blank and do not build further on previous experience and knowledge, which would help to design new smart contract applications and to implement smart contracts in existing applications.

Governmental services

Governmental institutions

Current roles and forms Governments are necessary to steer organizations and citizens to achieve goals that can only be reached when governed from above, such as for example providing electricity, reducing climate change, subsidizing museums, or limiting the sales of tobacco and alcohol for minors. Without these institutions, people with different goals and ideas would constantly fight each other. Governments need to provide citizens and organizations with trust in the future in order to work, invest, and consume, which stimulates welfare and wellbeing. But the term government is used for many institutions. The definition, according to the Oxford dictionary, is "the group of people with the authority to govern a country or state." This definition would imply that the government is only on a regional or national level, but governmental institutions appear on many levels. These can differ per country, but the most common levels are: supranational (for example, the European Union), national, regional (for example, the state of Ohio), and local (municipalities).

Within each of these levels, there are activities that the government performs by having interactions with other parties.

Governmental services can be divided into four different types of interactions:

• Government-to-government – Interaction between governmental institutions;

• Government-to-business – Interaction between governmental institutions and businesses;

• Government-to-citizen – Interaction between governmental institutions and citizens;

• Citizen-to-citizen – Interaction between citizens, which are facilitated by governments.

Governmental institutions are thus interacting with businesses and citizens in order to create trust and let businesses and citizens achieve goals together. The role of the third party that connects parties and provides services for citizens also gives much power to the government, which enlarges the need for non-corrupt and efficient governments. Large bureaucratic governments can still have large overhead costs. It can be said that "manufacturing trust can be expensive."

Effect of blockchain and smart contracts

It is said that blockchain has "the potential to improve all facets of government." Because the government is a large-scale bureaucratic organization, there is much to improve on terms of efficiency, friction, and costs. Improving governmental services by making them faster and more efficient, surely is desirable.

The foundations of blockchain technology were laid in the 1980s and 1990s. Several computer coders and mathematicians united in a group called the Cypherpunks. In a manifesto, they made clear their intentions: "These developments will alter completely the nature of government regulation, the power to tax and control economic interactions, the ability to keep information secret, and will even change the nature of trust and reputation.… The State will, of course, try to slow or halt the spread of this technology." A major implication of blockchain is the free use of cryptocurrencies. While national governments can confiscate money from your local (and central) bank account, this is not possible with for example Bitcoin, as the money is registered as decentralized and not controlled by one party. Digital payments are examples of a blockchain development that the government can only partially control. Governments can prevent the conversion of conventional money to cryptocurrencies through banks. However, the possession of cryptocurrencies is difficult to track. They can be stored offline and untraceable with a cold wallet. Payments are made through the decentralized and pseudonymous network, which makes banning payments difficult.

It is possible that some services heavily rely on governmental institutions at the moment, but will become mainly decentralized with blockchain. An example is identification, which already has blockchain technology partially implemented in Estonia. Estonia issues electronic identities (e-ID) for anyone who wants to. This is not limited to inhabitants of Estonia, because it does not grant citizenship. It does, though, enable owners of the e-ID to perform online commercial activities, like "business and company registration, opening of bank accounts and funds transfers, buying and selling of real estate and other property, and trade of goods and services." All those activities are not audited by a governmental institution, but by the blockchain network. Instead of the executor of the process, the government becomes merely the facilitator of the process. Where citizens used to have to trust the government, they can now trust the network. This, however, does not rule out governmental organizations.

Though the transactions are performed by the network, it is likely that the government "will set-up, execute, and maintain these architectures." Concluding, governmental services have many potential benefits from blockchain technology: faster, more secure, less costly, and with less friction. But the role of governmental institutions can change as well. In some examples, like land registration and identification, they could become merely the facilitator of the network instead of the controlling third party.

FINANCIAL TECHNOLOGY

The first to embrace blockchain technology were banks, governments, and other financial institutions, which are also users of the fast-growing blockchain. Powerful tools developed to manage and transfer money are redefining our world in an unexpected and new way. Therefore, it is logical that financial technology (fintech) becomes important. This section gives you an overview of current government activities in blockchain technology and how they affect you. Financial technology touches your daily life, whether you realize it or not.

Get Your Crystal Ball: Future Banking Trends

The banking sector was the first sector to recognize the threat of Bitcoin, then the potential of blockchain to transform the sector. The finance sector is highly regulated, and the costs of organizing and operating as a bank are high. These stringent regulations provide an insulation and protective shield for the entire industry as well as load. Applying fast and efficient digital money that does not support the cost of processing cash and is recognizable as it moves through the financial system was a powerful and threatening proposition. The idea that value can be kept out of the control of central governments has also aroused the interest of financial institutions and governments that support cryptocurrencies. Originally, these monetary institutions and governments tried to regulate blockchain regulation. Today, they are adopting blockchain by investing in all areas.

In 2013 and 2014, the United States alerted the Securities and Exchange Commission (SEC) to the possible risks associated with investing in virtual currency. The debate was that investors could be misled by the promise of high returns and would not be skeptical enough about new and innovative technology-led investment spaces. According to the SEC, digital currency was one of the top 10 threats to investors. Today, the SEC is ready to communicate with companies and investors that cryptocurrency is growing in all sectors. Not two years later, countries around the world, the United Kingdom, Canada, Australia, and China began looking for ways to create their own digital currency, seize cryptocurrencies, and market it. Money in the blockchain. The turning point was the time they began to realize that the benefits outweighed the risks. Bitcoin can resist hackers for many years, even when many government systems are compromised, making it an attractive system to try out. Blockchain's technological innovations have promised to manage billions of transactions to support economies, making large cryptocurrency feasible.

Blockchains are permanent, and there are immutable records of each transaction. Placing a country's money supply in a blockchain controlled by a central bank would have a significant impact on the fact that there will be a permanent record of all existing financial transactions at a particular level at a certain level in its blockchain record. Though they will not be visible to the public. Blockchain technology and digital currencies could reduce risk and fraud and give them maximum control over monetary policy and taxes. It would not be as anonymous as Bitcoin was at the beginning. In fact, on the contrary, it would allow them to keep a complete and verifiable track of every digital transaction carried out by individuals and businesses. This could even allow central banks to replace the functions of commercial banks in the circulation of money.

The question of the future of the banking sector can be daunting and exciting. Consumers can now pay their friends over the phone almost instantly in almost any type of currency or cryptocurrency. Increasingly retail stores are using cryptocurrencies to pay for goods and accept customer payments. In Kenya, the use of cryptocurrency is normal. However, this is still not a current option in most countries. Western markets are still in the early stages of adoption. Because most people associate their wealth with a legal tender issued by governments or with assets belonging to existing state systems, fintech innovations must merge with these existing systems before we can see the usefulness or classic currencies of the digital blockchain. If regulators find ways to tax and record accounts, there will be a massive adoption of a portfolio of customers with digitized tokens in two or three years.

The B2B market will start using blockchain much faster. A reinforced manufacturing system with associated policies and operations is available in less than two years. Ripple and R3, among other things, have worked hard to make this possible. These systems will be the first axis of institutional creation of digitized deposit representations. These are acknowledgments of debt between internal organizational departments and between trusted partners as suppliers. Regulators, central banks, and monetary authorities are investing a lot to make this possible. Canada and Singapore are moving very fast in this direction.

Regulations Know Your Client (KYC) and Anti-Money Laundering (AML) require banks to know who they are dealing with and to ensure that they are not involved in money laundering or terrorism. Cryptocurrency banks continue to face significant challenges. In accordance with KYC and AML regulations, they must know the identity of all the people who use their currency. In several cases, people's bank accounts are already debit and credit operations, such as bookkeeping books distributed in blockchains, with the exception of centralized accounts. The first candidates in this area will be regions where regulatory bodies, banks, and central banks work together. Singapore and Dubai are good candidates who already have blockchain initiatives.

The estimation of the volume of transactions had to be met by a blockchain that controls the currency of an economy like the United Kingdom or the United States, though it's difficult. The United States alone does billions of transactions a day, estimated at more than $ 17 billion a year. Lots of responsibility for new technology! A nation would be paralyzed if its money supply were threatened. The World Bank, the International Monetary Fund, the Bank for International Settlements, and central banks around the world have decided to talk about blockchain technology. The first step towards a faster and cheaper currency would be to adopt the blockchain as a protocol to facilitate bank transfers and interbank settlement. The official digital currencies would become more accepted over time. Individual consumers are aware of the reduced costs associated with using blockchain for interbank contracts. The savings will be seen in the bank's net results as a reduction in the costs associated with the fees charged by intermediaries.

Consumers will always want branches and commercial banks in the near future. But Generation Y has already accepted enabled payments through PayPal, Venmo, Cash, and more. A new payment method on their phones will put them in a phase. The big challenge is that if all the money is digital, compromising it can be disastrous. It is possible that the blockchain architecture is powerful enough to overcome the problem related to the unexpected code execution in the system, which occurred during the hacking of DAO (Autonomously Decentralized Organization) in Ethereum. Had cryptocurrency worked in a traditional public blockchain, 51% of network nodes would have agreed to the solution. Obtaining an agreement can be time-consuming and appropriate for businesses and people who need stable and secure money at all times. Many blockchains function as democracies. Most (51%) of the network blockchain nodes were subject to change.

Blockchains will pave the way for many new types of securities and investment products. New markets will open up with more efficient methods of calculating risk, as guarantees will be much more transparent and flexible across institutions when reflected in a mass return system.

It is possible that countries that can release their dead capital, real estate that they cannot finance, and groups can sell their shares in these assets in the global market. This would include, for example, transparent mortgage-backed securities for the development of new real estate in Colombia or Peru. In the future, countries may release their dead capital. Owners of real estate, undeveloped land, and non-bank property can now sell interest on these assets in the global market. These assets will be attractive because asset managers can actively analyze low-performing assets, given the transparency and capability of the entity replaced by blockchain-based technology. Using blockchains to manage these assets will give managers the power to always own the best-performing stocks, eliminate rotten apples, reclassify them, and sell them as new titles.

For non-institutional clients, micro-investment will be an attractive opportunity, globally and locally activated, through blockchain trading platforms. The use of blockchain technology will also provide them with the means to invest in companies and their specific activities without being minimal or passing intermediaries that absorb a percentage of the investment.

With the present structure of blockchains, the customer is liable for his very own security. At present, clients don't have the principal weight of shielding and safeguarding themselves from misfortune. Bigger companies and governments offer protection and security, and they have for whatever length of time that anybody can recall. Ordinary individuals haven't needed to secure themselves thusly since they quit holding their own gold during medieval times (pretty much).

Ensured installments that are allowed through blockchain-backed transactions will build trade in places where trust is low. Less fortunate countries can contend on a similar playing field as wealthier countries inside these kinds of systems. As this occurs throughout the following ten years, the worldwide economies will move. The expense of items and work may increase. Worldwide companies pay their workers dependent on focused evaluating, just as on representatives' past pay rates. Designers and other knowledge workers would be the exemption because it'll be simpler for them to help themselves dependent on mysterious work.

Monetary consideration and equivalent worldwide trade are important points for governments. The selection of computerized monetary standards will more likely be done nationwide in small and developing countries. Most large countries have decentralized power structures that prevent fast changes to indispensable systems like cash. Their focal power structures of small countries will enable them to hurdle over traditional infrastructure and organization. For example, generally, African and South American countries don't have landlines or addresses, yet they all have smartphones and the capacity to make cryptocurrency wallets. The missing piece is generally speaking trade liquidity and capacity to pay for fundamental needs, for example, utilities, lease, and food through a cryptocurrency.

REAL ESTATE

The real estate sector will be one of the industries most affected by innovations in blockchain technology. The effect will be felt in each country in a slightly different way. In the Western world, there may be benefits such as transparent mortgage-backed securities that are traded on blockchain compatible exchanges. Blockchain integration already exists in China, especially with notarization, which is an essential component of real estate transactions. In developing countries, blockchains are the most promising because they can free up capital and increase trade.

This section analyzes innovations in the real estate world around the world. I also inform you of possible future changes and important implications of blockchain technology. The real estate sector holds much of the world's wealth and economic stability. The industry will grow very quickly in the coming years, and it will be helpful to know where these changes will happen and how you and your business can benefit.

Elimination of ownership rights

Property insurance compensates for financial losses due to damage to your title while purchasing a property. It is necessary if you are taking out a mortgage from your home or refinancing. Property insurance protects a bank's investment against property rights issues that may not be in the public domain, are omitted in the search for titles, or are the result of fraud or forgery. Ownership is necessary in common law countries to operate their value systems. The buyer is responsible for ensuring that the seller has a good title. These systems search for titles and buy insurance. In areas using the Torrens title system, the buyer can rely on the real estate registry data and must go beyond that. Blockchain technology has been proposed as an adjunct to assist consumers in customary value systems. The idea is simple: blockchains are fantastic public filing systems; they were also considered obsolete or modified without registration. Theoretically, blockchains could transform common law systems into value-sharing systems in Torrens.

First, however, many challenges must be overcome. In the common law system, each county has its own land register, which records and registers all deeds or records transferring land ownership or any interest in the county's land. The United States alone has thousands of counties. Thousands of individual offices create databases. Changes to the on-site blockchain or the way records are organized. New laws must be created to dictate that all interest and land transfers must be registered in the system in order to be valid. So, only Torrens's blockchain system and technology can make it redundant. An exception would be in areas where there is a lot of property transfer register. In the following sections, we will explore the real estate sector and the areas where blockchains add value.

Protected industries

Every industry creates systems to keep new competition out. It may be a high administrative weight, government-allowed restraining infrastructures, or high startup costs. The industry that has built up around the buying and selling of real domain hasn't changed much over the last 40 years and is ready for disturbance. A wide range of parties adds to the process. Here are the various industries that are built around the buying and selling of homes:

Real estate operators: a realtor encourages you to look at changed neighborhoods and locate a home. He regularly encourages you to negotiate a price and speaks with the seller for your sake. This administration is significant, and it's not prone to be displaced by blockchain technology. You would already be able to buy a home without a realtor— people decide to work with them because they improve the process.

Home inspectors: home inspectors reveal defects with the house before you buy it — defects that could cost you money in the near future. The defects home inspectors find can be used to negotiate with the seller at a superior cost. In the future, homes will keep on having mileage — that will never show signs of change. So, blockchain technology could be used to record fixes to property and defects found in the investigation.

Closing agents: at closing, the last step is the settlement. The closing agent oversees and arranges the closing documents, records them, and discharges the money to the fitting parties. Closing agents might be displaced by blockchain technology — the tasks performed by closing representatives could be built into smart contracts or chaincode.

Mortgage lenders and servicers: mortgage lenders and servicers provide assets for a mortgage and gather the progressing mortgage installments. They won't be displaced with blockchain software; however, they may use blockchain technology to assist them with lessening costs with recordkeeping and investigating.

Real estate appraisers: the real estate appraiser's main responsibility is to take a look at a property and decide how much it's value. The examination process is done each time a property is purchased or renegotiated. Companies like Zillow have taken a great deal of the legwork out of realizing the market value. Yet, each home is unique and needs to be evaluated intermittently. Indeed, even in the real estate mortgage process, various interests might be called for to meet everybody's needs. It may be useful to record this data inside a blockchain as a public witness.

Loan officers: loan officers use your credit, money related, and work information to check whether you fit the bill for a mortgage. They at that point, coordinate what you're eligible for with products that they sell. Like a realtor, a loan officer encourages you to get the best choice across a range of choices. Blockchain software might be used to help loan officers monitor documents that they give you and review the process for reasonable lending law compliance.

Loan processors: a loan processor helps loan officers in planning mortgage loan information and the application for introduction to the underwriter. Software that pulls the buyer's source information is being investigated. It's not blockchain technology, yet it could be problematic for this position.

Mortgage underwriters: a mortgage underwriter decides if you're eligible for a mortgage loan. She approves or dismisses your mortgage loan application dependent on your record as a consumer, business, assets, and obligations. Organizations are investigating robotizing the underwriting process utilizing man-made reasoning. However, it's not blockchain technology.

Every one of these operators fills a need that secures the buyer, seller, and mortgage provider. In many industries, the cost of working together goes down after some time — improvements in proficiency achieved by competition and advancement add to driving down cost. The mortgage industry is appealing as a candidate for blockchain advancement because the inverse has happened: the cost of business has gone up. The average U.S. mortgage is more than 500 pages and costs $7,500 to start. This is three times what it cost ten years prior. Blockchain technology can meet the needs of protecting the buyer, seller, and mortgage provider while decreasing the cost to do so.

Mortgages in the Blockchain World

A mortgage in a blockchain world won't appear that entirely different than a mortgage in the customary world. The part that you'll see is that a blockchain mortgage will be more affordable at closing. Given that the vast majority just ever buy a couple of homes in their lifetimes, the distinction may not appear to be a serious deal. In any case, the money adds up. Blockchain technology could bring down the cost to originate a mortgage back to pre-2007 levels.

Diminishing your origination costs

Mortgage origination costs have expanded, and the explanation is basic: banks fear fines that they can cause If they mess up any part of the mortgage process. In this way, the industry has placed steps to help ensure that they meet every one of the requirements at the time of origination and years after the fact when they're evaluated. Huge banks have paid billions in fines from the mishandling of documents. They're presently required not exclusively to have all the fundamental documents, yet in addition to proving that they pursued the right process and sent all the important documents to you. Blockchain-based products reduce the repetition that banks started joining into their process after the downturn.

Recordkeeping and auditing expenses have soared since the presentation of the Dodd–Frank Wall Street Reform and Consumer Protection Act, and blockchain technology could reduce that cost. Companies needing to meet the needs of banks with a blockchain solution would need to give banks a chance to prove that they pursued the guidelines set out in Dodd–Frank. It would likewise assist banks with documenting why they made certain choices on loans, and assist them with finding documents that were used originally, regardless of whether they aren't in control of them.

Blockchain applications could put near $4,000 back on the table for the normal home purchase. The mortgage industry is a ton like the car loan industry and the Visa industry. Comparative applications could reduce the administration cost that these industries have because of consumer protection laws, while simultaneously giving companies a chance to meet those requirements.

Knowing your last-known document

One of the biggest cost drivers in the mortgage origination process regularly comes years after the loan was first made. Sometimes those encouraging the loan process include unneeded documents into client files or old files that aren't used to originate a loan are left in the organizer. Likewise, copying of records may happen. At the point when it comes time to review the file, there is an excessive amount of information to filter through. Banks pay money to outside firms to check their records and attempt to figure out what documents were used in the last dismemberment on your loan. Blockchain software can take care of this issue in an exquisite manner. Blockchains are distributed recordkeeping systems that take into account various parties to collaborate on data after some time without forgetting about what that data resembled at some random point en route. This means the half dozen individual organizations that collaborate to assist you with buying your home can now all interact on a similar chain.

The chain in this case would start with you. Your channel will eventually add sub-channels, such as buying a home. Then you can authorize other people: banks, employers, credit bureaus, valuation companies, etc. Each would add their own information to their channel, and the other authorized parties could read that information and add their own. Blockchains would change the need for a central file repository. This would automate part of the document processing and always provide a clear history of your loan, reducing the need to check and prepare your documents for confirmation. It's a great idea, but the whole ecosystem will have to work together. Each branch would strengthen the system and provide added value, somewhat similar to the way each additional person faxed it to another utility.

INSURANCE

Blockchain insurance technology is designed to change the way people and businesses buy and receive insurance, and they arrive faster than you think! You need to recognize the implications of these new technologies on the horizon.

In this section, we will see how executing blockchain contracts independently shape corporate policy and structure. It prepares you for fundamental technological changes that can change the burden of proof. After reading this section, you can make more informed decisions about insurance coverage and blockchain-based payments. You will understand how the coverage price will affect you and the different types of coverage that will be available to you in the future.

IoT devices, immutable data, decentralized autonomous organizations (CAD), and smart contracts are changing the evolution of consumer insurance. The union of all these technologies is possible thanks to the development of blockchain.

Blockchains are doing some very good things that will allow for two major changes in the way you buy and sell insurance: people will be able to get more personalized coverage, and new markets will open up as soon as costs were not possible.

Secure the individual

Security built around an individual will allow a significant change in priorities. Asset management will be less critical, and insurers can focus on calculating the risk and adequacy of supply and demand. You can create a marketing platform that guarantees customers. There are several ways to organize this new activity. One option would be an on-demand market where users post their requests, either standardized by a personalized smart contract or a Chaincode contract.

As an insurer, with this type of model, you can calculate a premium for specific demand based on historical data and other risk calculation factors for your risk model. If the customer is satisfied with the proposal, they can offer or subscribe, depending on the application model used. This new type of insurance could be adopted by peer-to-peer (P2P) or crowdfunding insurance or by a traditional insurance company that has embraced the technology. In both cases, they are both created in a decentralized cryptocurrency registry using smart contracts/chaincode, which guarantees the payment of the client to the investor and vice versa in the event of an incident. Blockchain is crucial because it allows for some operations that were impossible to protect to be protected now.

Blockchains generate value transfers without any friction, which means that micro-rims are achievable because transaction rates are very low. You can now open new markets without a monetary system or a legal operating system, or in cases where transaction and litigation costs outweigh the benefits offered. You can use CAD smart contracts to manage large groups at a fraction of the cost and time. You can use this template to include and manage your new business and possibly crowdfunding insurance platforms. The automatic nature of smart contracts could also shed light on the many costs associated with third-party claims and adjustments that contribute to processing and fundraising.

The legality of all this is always in doubt. Issues of confidentiality and consumer rights are difficult to identify. The state also has its own regulations and information. However, when these regulations are complied with, insurance experience and consumer insurance will change significantly.

GOVERNMENT

In this section, we will look at exciting innovations that are taking place within governments and companies that support them with innovative blockchain ventures. Everyday business is affected by scams and fraud, and this section explains how governments are fighting back against identity theft and cybercrime. You also find out about smart cities initiatives that will be critical to economic growth and sustainability – many using blockchain technology to bridge technological gaps.

The smart cities of Asia

Smart cities take advantage of modern technologies to improve infrastructure and security, as well as improve traffic and air quality. Becoming a smart city is flourishing, and almost all major municipalities have embraced the concept of a smart city. Blockchain is particularly useful when integrated with the Internet of Things (IoT) used by smart cities. Currently, several interesting projects for commercial employment are being tested. The United States Department of Homeland Security is investigating IoT devices used by Customs and Border Protection (CBP). Companies like Slock.it allow affiliate facilities to use blockchain to make smart contracts. Its first product was a blockchain-compatible smart lock that can be used by Airbnb customers. Integrating these technologies enables devices to use their sensors to establish smart contracts. The same technology could be used in city parking meters.

Blockchain technology can also be used to securely exchange information between networks in a smart city. Numerous cities are exploring how to use blockchain to reduce congestion. Singapore's Smart Nation project hopes to measure the conditions of their bus journeys using the mobile phones of its citizens and then analyze the data to determine when roads need improvement. Singapore is a leader in smart city development and has started developing smart cities in other countries.

The battle for the financial capital of the world.

Blockchain technology grew out of public awareness with a lot of news in 2015. Since then, many new businesses have worked in beta and pre-released versions. In the span of one night, nearly 2000 new startups were formed. It has been introduced in 2017 and 2018 in markets in Singapore, Dubai, and London, where regulators welcome innovation and compete to become the world's financial mecca. This is for fintech leaders and smart cities. There is a race for relevance in a world that is evolving towards the citizens of a borderless and financially fluid world.

In 2016, the UK government released a report entitled *"Distributed Book Technology: Beyond the Blockchain Network"* (https://goo.gl/asIz6L), arguing that the book blockchain technology of books) could be used to reduce corruption, error, and fraud and makes different processes more efficient. They also said that blockchains could change the attitude of citizens towards their government by providing greater transparency and reliability. But London has been very familiar with technology since at least 2014. Many new Blockchain companies have been established or operated in the UK as it was the safest unofficial place to start a business. At the time, this was a big problem as many cryptocurrency entrepreneurs were arrested in 2014 and 2015.

Since the release of this report, blockchains have been approved in the UK, including Whitehall divisions (non-divisional departments such as the Land Registry, Forestry Commission, and Food Standards), local authorities, and delegated governments.

Here are some interesting projects and experiences in the UK:

• Blockchain-based social assistance distribution: The Ministry of Labor and Pensions has partnered with Barclays, RWE, GovCoin, and the University of London for an experimental social welfare distribution technology experiment. With the phone app, there was a test aimed to determine if payment could be sent and monitored using blockchain technology.

• DLT Government: Credits, the blockchain platform provider, and the UK government are collaborating on a framework for UK government agencies to experiment with blockchain technology. (DLT stands for Distributed Book Technology).

• International blockchain payments: Santander Bank has launched an international blockchain payment test. The staff pilot program includes an app that is linked to Apple Pay. Customers can use the Touch ID to transfer payments between £ 1,000 and £

10,000.

• Using blockchain technology to trade gold: Royal Mint has partnered with CME Group, a commercial operator, to use blockchain technology to create a gold market in the hopes of turning London into gold; a more attractive city for selling gold. Blockchain technology is being adopted by both entities because they see it as an effective digital mechanism for trading gold.

Overall Effect of Blockchain on Human Life

With all of the media set aflame with news of prices of cryptocurrencies, you may ask yourself how it affects a common man. At the center of cryptocurrency and other digital currencies is Blockchain technology.

There are numerous industrial and administrative obstacles that technology can solve for the ordinary man. Do you own a small business but repeatedly feel transparency is missing due to traditional procedures of communication? As a business owner, is finding legitimate job applicants a hassle for you? Have you ever found yourself battling with higher than usual medical bills? These problems affect entrepreneurs, small businesses, startups, individuals alike, and Blockchain technology aims to deliver solutions to make the life of a common man so much easier through simplified solutions.

Banking

In almost all countries, banking is still focused on paper-intensive transactions for any money transfer, recordkeeping, or other important functions. Blockchain technology can copy this digitally and create a decentralized registry that allows not only bankers but also customers to access a unique source of information. This system allows banks to eliminate the possibility of fraud, as bankers in the Blockchain registry can numerically check the documentation and proof of ownership of assets, which are available at all times in a consistent form.

Identity theft is also a major problem in the banking sector as citizen information is stolen and used to open fraudulent accounts for illegal activities. According to the Federal Trade Complaints Database, more than 13 million complaints were filed against card fraud and identity theft, and 3 million of these complaints were filed in 2016. Through the blockchain system, users can directly view all accounts on their behalf and immediately notify their banks in case they detect suspicious activity in their bank details. Some well-known examples include IBM's compatible Hyperledger Fabric project and the UBS Settlement Coin utility.

Healthcare

Blockchain technology can dramatically streamline medical care and streamline medical data management. If the widespread availability of patient records can make research suitable for medication use and minimize the effects of counterfeit medicines, clinical trials and their results may be available in a decentralized network that enables healthcare professionals and researchers to conduct research and find solutions for better medical care. Accenture is one of the largest companies to begin offering innovative healthcare solutions for the healthcare industry for secure fraud-free transactions.

Health insurance fraud can also be eliminated through blockchain billing management, as the billing system can be fully automated, without any room for fraudulent intermediary activity. With more than 56 million people on Medicare in 2017, more than $ 1.3 billion was taken from the government through fraudulent activities in rehab facilities and home care services. Blockchain systems can effectively protect citizens seeking medical attention from healthcare providers who charge additional fees for services offered through fraudulent billing procedures. Centralized data not only helps healthcare professionals deliver treatment based on patient and family history but also eliminates the risk of the patient misreading past symptoms or disorders.

Public Records

One of the most important civic administration functions of a government is to track record all information about its citizens. This consists of information about individuals and businesses with regards to their assets and activities. Most of the documented information is documented in paper databases, making data management exceedingly difficult even in developed countries.

Blockchain-based systems like Ubitiquity can encrypt all public records in a digital archive to keep the data on citizens from being altered for fraudulent activities. Identity theft is an issue that can be quite challenging to deal with for the administration, and digitizing all public information to render them tamper-proof can help prevent such instances of criminal endeavors.

Voting

One of the biggest shortcomings of the voting system in almost every country is that even in the present day, voters need to be physically present at polling booths to cast their votes; this can make things difficult for people who need to travel on poll days. Most importantly, the average citizen has no means of verifying the poll results.

Blockchain development companies like Followmyvote are going to come up with solutions that seek to make online voting the new normal. It will permit citizens to view accurate information on poll standings and results and various other data publicly. It also leads to safer voting for citizens of countries in external or internal conflict, and criminal activities to force citizens into voting for specific candidates can be wholly avoided.

Business Hiring

Businesses of all sizes have a difficult time finding the correct staff. Through blockchain technology, it is feasible for businesses to confirm certifications of all candidates through an advanced database. Blockchain technology can be applied to make a decentralized database of experts with checked capabilities in a protected record that businesses can allude to for hiring up-and-comers. Learning Machine is a New-York based organization that looks to address this issue centers around recording undeniable information on workers.

Expense or work-related cheats make up 34% of all identity theft starting in 2016, and a blockchain system makes the hiring process for any business significantly more secure as an organization would approach substantial up-and-comers just, diminishing the danger of hiring deceitful representatives. It likewise enables candidates by accelerating the hiring process and helping them to secure positions they are qualified for and have a problem-free application process.

Utilization of blockchain innovations helps people and businesses the same, and it additionally secures individual information while making important data freely obvious. While blockchain has the best application in cryptographic money, its utilization can spread to different sectors also to provide important answers for residents around the globe.

At long last, the trading of money, much the same as medical research, requires an elevated level of trust. Money in the past has created this trust through government guidelines and national bank oversight. Medical research in the past has endeavored to make elevated levels of trust through friend survey led by trustworthy medical diaries, for example, the New England Journal of Medicine. The two methods of producing trust depend on a trusted focal authority, either the administration or a medical diary. All things considered, the two methods are exceptionally defenseless to misrepresentation by means of corruption or honest errors of the brought together authority. This has prompted across the board distrust in medical research. Bitcoin works in an unexpected way since it sets up a strategy for depending on a conveyed network dependent on a numerical algorithm, as opposed to human error.

Monetary exchanges require maybe the most significant level of trust. Individuals need to realize that all exchanges recorded in the record be completely exact and absolutely impervious to being changed later on. Since blockchain technology, as actualized in bitcoin, has earned this trust, bitcoin has become a generally utilized store of significant value with a market capitalization of over $100 billion USD. At the point when different cryptographic forms of money are considered, the all-out trust in blockchain-based budgetary systems surpasses $250 billion USD. Thus, human services experts should have the option to trust that data acquired from medical research is both totally precise and totally changeless. Doctors need to realize that medical research isn't copied or deceitful in any capacity. Blockchain technology has made bitcoin a trusted, worldwide cash. Similarly, blockchain-based medical research will enormously build trust in the outcomes and, subsequently, improved medical consideration.

LIMITATIONS

It can be said without exaggeration that it is a masterpiece of the genius mind. However, blockchain is not perfect or not limited. Therefore, this step highlights and explains the major limitations of the blockchain and explains why these restrictions create significant barriers to its commercial use.

Challenge

Blockchain is a purely distributed point-to-point system that allows everyone to read transaction history and add new transaction data to the data collection. The opening and absence of any form of centralized control or coordination are at the heart of the system, as it enables its nodes to act as independent witnesses and clarify owner issues. However, openness and lack of central control can have undesirable consequences that limit the use of the system. The challenge is to recognize and understand the consequences of the system by ordering strategies to overcome them.

Technical Limitations of the Blockchain

The most important technical limitations of the blockchain are:

• Lack of privacy

• The security model

• Limited scalability

- High costs

- Hidden centrality

- Lack of flexibility

- Critical size

Lack of Privacy

The Blockchain is a large, cleanly distributed peer-to-peer book that stores the entire history of transaction data. All details of the transaction, such as the assets and the amount transferred, the accounts involved, and the date of the transfer, are available to everyone. This is necessary to allow each party to clean up the entity and check for new transactions (for example, identifying a double-spend incident). Therefore, lack of privacy is an integral part of the blockchain. Without this level of transparency, the blockchain would not be able to fulfill its duty. However, this level of transparency is often considered as a limiting factor for filing cases that require greater confidentiality.

The Security Model

The blockchain uses asymmetric cryptography to identify, authenticate users, and authorize transactions. Blockchain account numbers are actually public cryptographic keys. Only the person who owns the appropriate private key can access the entity associated with the account. Only transaction information that contains a digital signature created with the appropriate private key and can transfer ownership from one account to another is relevant.

The private key is the major security instrument that enables the rightful owner. As soon as a private account key is handed to another person, intentionally, accidentally, by mistake or theft, the security of that individual account is compromised.

No additional security measures protect the assets associated with the account number. It is important to remember that asymmetric cryptography used in blockchain is considered one of the best available cryptographic methods. Therefore, the concept of blockchain security, as such, is neither faulty nor deficient. However, there is no additional security network to protect blockchain users from unwanted loss or sharing of their private key with others. They are similar to how real-life security keys are used to protect homes or cars, or how PINs are used to protect credit or debit cards. Once you give someone a key, no matter what the circumstances or reason, security is broken, and anyone with a PIN or key can withdraw money from your credit card or drive your car. The blockchain account's private key does not avoid this. However, some believe that the lack of additional security measures is a limiting factor for the use of blockchain.

Limited Scalability

A blockchain is a system that has two goals: one above the other, it allows everyone to add new transaction data to a shared managed history. On the other hand, it protects transaction history information from unauthorized access or forgery. Blockchain balances two goals using an immutable data structure composed solely of sums, which requires a puzzle solution each time a new block is added. Solving this puzzle voluntarily takes a long time. Insisting on a puzzle is a convenient way to make expensive attempts to manipulate transaction history data. Unfortunately, this security measure results in a reduction in processing speed, and hence limited scalability. This blockchain feature is considered a major barrier to use in contexts that require high processing speed, high scalability, and high performance.

High Costs

The issue of high costs is linked to the problem of limited scalability. Solve a hash puzzle or take a quick labor cost test to calculate. This is a security measure that makes transaction history unchanged. Calculation costs can be expressed on various scales, such as the number of cycles of calculation, physical time, electricity, and money. However, the result is always the same: proof of work is expensive. As a result, the entire blockchain has costs. The size of these costs depends on the weight of the hash puzzles.

Hidden Centrality

The necessity to comprehend a hash puzzle for each square being added to the blockchain-data-structure and the principles for circulating prizes for contributing to the integrity of the system cause a race of arms among the peers. The individuals who have the essential budgetary assets put resources into specialist hardware that makes settling the hash puzzle and thus contributing to the system rewarding. Then again, the endeavor of approving and adding new exchange data to the system comes unfruitful for those without access to specialist hardware, which as a result, makes them pull back from contributing computational assets to the system. Accordingly, the apparently huge and different group of peers keep up the integrity of the system, in the long run, turns into an extremely small group of entities that each possesses colossal computational power as specialist hardware. The rest of the group of peers forms an oligopoly that partitions the duty of keeping up the integrity of the system among themselves. Like oligopolies in different businesses, this small group of entities could manhandle its capacity (e.g., by precluding explicit exchanges or segregating explicit users). This impact builds up a sort of concealed centrality that undermines the circulated idea of the entire system. From a specialized perspective, such a system is as yet an appropriated system, yet it is a system whose integrity is kept up by just a small number of entities.

Lack of Flexibility

The blockchain is a complex technological construct that is comprised of a variety of concepts and procedures that are optimized and adapted to one another. Altering that fine-tuned ecosystem can be very challenging. Essentially, there is no established procedure for how to change or upgrade major components of a blockchain once it has begun its operation. This implicitly creates a long service life for the technologies that make up the blockchain. For instance, the cryptographic procedures have to be valid for the lifetime of the blockchain, which is potentially centuries. This is also true for the blockchain-algorithm and how conflicts are resolved. There is also a problem for people developing the blockchain further due to immutability, in that it is hard to fix bugs or make any modifications to the blockchain protocol. These characteristics make the whole blockchain-technology-suite less flexible than other technologies.

Critical Size

The strength against manipulations and hence the trustworthiness of the collectively maintained history of transaction data rely on the premise that the majority of the system's computational power is controlled by honest nodes. Still, in small peer-to-peer systems with restricted computational power, that majority can still be very small, which in turn could make it possible to execute a 51 percent attack. This problem is, in particular, relevant for cryptocurrencies with low stock market value and limited user adoption. Therefore, any blockchain will require a critical mass of honest nodes to support it and make it resistant to attackers with a lot of computational power. Reaching a critical size that makes 51 percent of attacks impossible is a challenge that every new blockchain has to face.

Nontechnical Limitations of the Blockchain

The most important nontechnical limitations of the blockchain are:

• Lack of legal acceptance

• Lack of user acceptance

Lack of Legal Acceptance

Blockchain is a technology that offers its users the ability to manage and transfer ownership in an open and cleanly distributed peer-to-peer system. How independent peers jointly manage assets through distributed consensus has raised doubts about the legal consequences of transactions executed and managed in the blockchain. Questions about the legal implications and acceptance of blockchain transactions need to be discussed regarding the security and sophistication of their technology. This is a question of incorporating a new approach to property management into the established legal system. Those who have witnessed the emergence and development of the Internet can see the similarity of blockchain legal statuses today and the lack of legal acceptance of online commerce in the 1990s.

Lack of User Acceptance

User acceptance, or a lack of it, is another limitation that cannot be underestimated. An open legal status of the blockchain will cause uncertainty among its users, which in turn will reduce their interest in using it. An additional aspect of user acceptance is knowledge and education. It is unrealistic to expect that customers will use and trust the blockchain when its fundamental functioning is not understood.

Overcoming the Limitations

Technical and non-technical constraints are considered important barriers to the adoption of blockchain in real-world applications. As certain constraints are overcome, there has been and remains an area of active research and further development. A detailed discussion of these activities goes beyond the scope of this book. However, the following sections explain how to overcome blockchain restrictions.

Technical limitations

Overcoming the technical limitations of the blockchain may require interventions at all components and at all technical levels. One of the major challenges to overcome the technical blockchain is the difference between improving its technology and its fundamental change. The next step will address this issue in more detail.

Non-technical limitations

The non-technical limitations of blockchain can be considered as social, economic, legal, and psychological aspects of adapting to new technology. Educational and legal initiatives can be considered as appropriate measures to control blockchain adoption. The example of the internet and e-commerce has already shown that it takes time to answer legal questions posed by new technologies and that it takes time for users to understand, trust, and use them. Fortunately, the case of the internet and e-commerce has also shown that educational initiatives on the work of new technologies increase user acceptance and adoption and help to solve legal problems.